A Pilgrimage to Jasna Góra

Portrait of Władysław Stanisław Reymont,
by Jacek Malczewski (15 July 1854–8 October 1929)

A Pilgrimage to
Jasna Góra
(Pielgrzymka do Jasnej Góry)

WŁADYSŁAW STANISŁAW
REYMONT

*Winner of the 1924 Nobel Prize in
Literature for* The Peasants (Chłopi)

Translated by
FILIP MAZURCZAK

Foreword by
MICHAŁ GOŁĘBIOWSKI

AROUCA
PRESS

First published in 1895 as
Pielgrzymka do Jasnej Góry
Copyright © by Arouca Press 2020
English Translation © Filip Mazurczak
Foreword © Michał Gołębiowski

Edited by Mary Frances Floody, Clarissa
Kwasniewski, and Genevieve Kwasniewski.

ISBN: 978-1-989905-15-9 (pbk)
ISBN: 978-1-989905-16-6 (hardcover)

Arouca Press
PO Box 55003
Bridgeport PO
Waterloo, ON N2J 3G0
Canada
www.aroucapress.com
Send inquiries to info@aroucapress.com

Book and cover design
by Michael Schrauzer
Cover image:
Alfons Karpiński, *Pilgrims*, 1907
oil, tempera on canvas,
From the collection of
the Regional Museum in Stalowa Wola
(Used with permission)

CONTENTS

LIST OF PHOTOGRAPHS

(PAGES 57–60)

Photo 1: Pilgrims in folk costume on the way from Łowicz to Częstochowa. May 22, 2010.

Photo 2: The 307th Walking Pilgrimage from Warsaw to Częstochowa. August 14, 2018. Credit: EpiskopatNews.

Photo 3: Cardinal Kazimierz Nycz, Archbishop of Warsaw, with Pauline fathers and pilgrims. August 14, 2018. Credit: EpiskopatNews.

Photo 4: The 27th Walking Pilgrimage from Zaolzie in Silesia. July 20, 2017.

Photo 5: Walking Pilgrimage from Wadowice, hometown of Pope St. John Paul II. July 19, 2017.

Photo 6: Pilgrims from Wadowice, hometown of Pope St. John Paul II, prostrating in front of Jasna Góra. July 19, 2017.

Photo 7: The 38th Pilgrimage of Defenders of Life. April 7, 2018.

Photo 8: 1987, during the Solidarity period. Banner reads: "Freedom, Love, Peace"

TRANSLATOR'S
FOREWORD

IT WAS SLIGHTLY MORE THAN A DECADE ago that I first heard that Władysław Reymont had written an account of his participation in a pilgrimage to Jasna Góra, when I read an article about the book in *Gość Niedzielny*, Poland's bestselling Catholic weekly.

I was very much intrigued, as Reymont was not known for writing on religious topics. Furthermore, as I myself have taken part in eight walking pilgrimages to Jasna Góra (two with the Archdiocese of Wrocław, one with the Archdiocese of Krakow, and five with the Dominican Order, whose starting point is also Krakow; I have spent a total of fifty-nine days on such pilgrimages) I was curious to see how different today's pilgrimages are from those in 1894.

The pilgrimage from Warsaw, which Reymont attended, is very old, having been held for the first time in 1711. In 1951, Poland's Stalinist government abolished all organized walking pilgrimages to Jasna Góra except for that from Warsaw as part of its aggressive program of state-sponsored atheism. After 1956, however, the regime became less repressive towards the Church, and eventually pilgrimages could be held once again.

Most other pilgrimages to Jasna Góra were initiated in the 1980s, especially in 1981, the year when Pope St. John Paul II narrowly survived an assassination attempt by Ali Ağca (almost certainly orchestrated by the KGB) and when Cardinal Stefan Wyszyński passed away — Poland's "Primate of the Millennium," known for his uncompromising attitude towards the communist regime, a kind of Moses who led the Polish nation across the desert of Marxist-Leninist tyranny. That summer, many Poles walked to Jasna Góra in order to express their thanks to God and Mary for saving the pope's life and for Wyszyński's heroic ministry.

During the Solidarity period of the 1980s, when the Church and especially John Paul II were closely affiliated with the anti-communist, pro-democratic movement, huge numbers of Poles walked to Jasna Góra. The popularity of such pilgrimages declined throughout the 1990s and 2000s, but in recent years there has been an increase in the number of Poles walking to the Marian shrine. In the summer of 2019, 133,000 pilgrims walked to Jasna Góra in 300 organized pilgrimages. Over the past few years, the popularity of novel kinds of pilgrimages to Jasna Góra—on bicycle, horseback, motorcycle, rollerblades, or by running—has rapidly grown.

Compared to Reymont's time, pilgrimages today are not only more numerous, they also offer more variety. Most are organized by dioceses and sometimes religious orders and are divided into smaller groups, many of which are directed towards a specific group of believers; for example, there are groups for university students (arguably the most common type), parents with small children, those who love the Latin Mass, and the members of the military. There is even a pilgrimage for hippies, which was founded by the late Father Andrzej Szpak, a Salesian priest. Some groups, especially the youth-oriented ones, are loud and sing joyful songs, while others are more solemn, reflective, and penitential in nature.

On a typical day during a pilgrimage to Jasna Góra, pilgrims wake up around five or six. Afterwards, Mass is celebrated. Pilgrims walk an average of about thirty kilometers (18.75 miles) a day and have three or four breaks at parishes. Most groups sing Lauds in the morning and Vespers in the evening; many also pray the Divine Mercy Chaplet at three in the afternoon. In the meantime, priests preach daily reflections, usually on that day's Scripture readings. In less solemn groups, pilgrims play the guitar and the whole company sings popular religious songs; several pilgrims volunteer to carry the amplifiers at each stretch that is walked.

As in Reymont's time, pilgrims to Jasna Góra today still customarily address one another as "brother" and "sister."

Pilgrims have the opportunity to confess to a priest just behind the rest of the procession. Every day, the rosary is said, and pilgrims have the opportunity to write down their intentions on slips of paper, which are later read in between decades (from my experience, a good husband is probably the most popular intention). At the front of each group, pilgrims carry a cross and banners with the group's name and logo.

Pilgrims spend the night in their own tents or in schools or fire stations. Sleeping at the homes of parishioners is becoming less common, however. During breaks, trucks sell food and drinks, and at some parishes where pilgrims stop to take five, parishioners serve soup, pasta, cake, and other food they have generously prepared.

Whereas most pilgrims who walk to Santiago de Compostela in Spain, for example, do not treat the pilgrimage as a religious event but more as something akin to a test of endurance, the religious aspect of walking pilgrimages to Jasna Góra is impossible to avoid. In my experience, virtually all pilgrims tend to be devout Catholics or at least those looking for God (and, occasionally, religiously apathetic men dragged by their more pious girlfriends).

However, there are also many opportunities for camaraderie and fun; the easy-to-learn "Belgian Dance," in which pilgrims dance in a circle (four steps forward, turn one hundred eighty degrees and four backwards, four forward, turn one hundred eighty degrees and four backwards, bring your partner closer and then away from you, spin your partner, and change partners) is a staple of breaks.

One of the great things about pilgrimages is the irresistible sense of community. In today's world which is increasingly hostile to the Christian faith, you can truly feel that there are many other dynamic young people who share your values.

I hope that my translation of *A Pilgrimage to Jasna Góra* will introduce the Anglophone reader to the writing of Władysław Reymont, who is sadly virtually forgotten outside Poland, and also to the wonderful tradition of pilgrimages to

Jasna Góra. For me, walking to the Black Madonna amidst the beauty of the Polish countryside in summer, which Reymont describes so sensuously, is the most important week of the year, something I impatiently await all year long.

Although *A Pilgrimage to Jasna Góra* is not a long work, translating it was at times difficult. Reymont was a very gifted writer, and I hoped to make sure that I conveyed the poetry of his language. Another challenging factor was the fact that the book was first published 125 years ago, and the Polish language has evolved greatly since then. Particularly difficult was the peasant dialect in some of the dialogue, which is archaic today and which was quite different from what one can read in most other Polish literature from the period, written by people from the higher strata of society. I would like to thank Michał Gołębiowski, the author of the foreword, for his assistance in some of the more challenging passages.

Filip Mazurczak
Wrocław
April 17, 2020

FILIP MAZURCZAK is a translator, journalist, and historian. He is a dual citizen of Poland and the United States and has spent many years of his life in both countries. His popular and academic articles have appeared in *First Things*, the *Catholic World Report*, *Polin: Studies in Polish Jewry*, and the *Oral History Review*.

FOREWORD

By Michał Gołębiowski

THE LIFE & WORK OF WŁADYSŁAW STANISŁAW REYMONT
Władysław Stanisław Reymont, laureate of the 1924 Nobel
Prize in Literature, has his place in the history of culture as
a great champion of the strength of the spirit. His greatest
literary accomplishment, the four-volume novel *The Peasants*, has been compared to the epic poetry of Hesiod and
Homer with the sole difference that Reymont's national epic
does not deal with major historical events, the meaning of
the history of the nation or the world, or even the heroic
deeds of revered kings and soldiers. Instead, *The Peasants*
presents the fate of an ordinary rural community. Reymont
was fascinated by human nature as interpreted through the
prism of "primordiality," of something that is timeless and
independent of the spirit of any individual moment in history. The domain of his prose was rural nature and the vigor
of human culture rather than artistic high society or urban
life. Another outstanding Polish writer of the same period,
Antoni Lange, accurately describes Reymont as follows:

> This was a man who had been brought up in an
> extra-historical world, in a rural environment,
> and who saw the life of his nation not against
> the backdrop of history, but against the backdrop
> of nature. This life was eternally uniform and
> revolved around the never-ending wheel of the
> four seasons of the year, but it was also full of
> hope in its fruitfulness and ceremonious solem-
> nity. There is no despair in Reymont. [...] He does
> not see that the nation strives for self-destruction
> because this nation has an element of persistence
> and self-preservation in its own vitality. Despite
> the primordiality of the spirit of this milieu,

Reymont discerns within it unvanquished obstinacy in the face of difficulties and breathes an epic cheerfulness. That is why he knew how to successfully grasp certain universal tones in the life of his nation and made his village of Lipce the window through which the whole world views Poland.[1]

In essence, the entirety of Reymont's literary legacy, especially the part that concerns descriptions of rural life, is saturated with the vigor of the spirit and a peculiar kind of fascination with human nature in which the author saw a constant struggle between two extremes. Human nature contains both a strong spiritual and transcendent element that aims for higher ideals as well as a relationship to the soil and a biological dimension, which pushes human life down to the level of the struggle for survival. This dualism is evident in the protagonists of Reymont's novels *The Comedienne* (alternate English title: *The Deceiver*) and *Ferments*, which describe the world of the artistic bohemia, but it is also present in the characters of the rural community depicted in *The Peasants*. They are all depicted as beings that belong equally to heaven and to earth, heroically displaying both angelic and contradictory animalistic traits. In any case, Reymont's life experiences shed light on this unique feature of his work.

Born on May 7, 1867, in Kobiele Wielkie as the son of a parish organist, from his youngest years Władysław Rejment (the original spelling of his name) above all displayed signs of being an innovative maverick. As a young boy, he refused to go to school and later frequently changed his profession and place of residence, constantly facing such challenges as poverty, rejection by the artistic milieu, or a railway accident. All these experiences tested the young writer's patience, and although in time they unexpectedly brought him numerous

---

1   A. Lange, *Pochodnie w mroku. Żeromski — Reymont — Kasprowicz*, Warsaw 1927, pp. 5–6.

benefits (for example, in the form of a very generous finan-
cial compensation for the train accident, thanks to which
Reymont could devote himself more fully to a literary career),
each time they strengthened his personality, making him a
tireless champion of the strong spirit.

In the 1880s, Reymont joined a theater troupe and hoped
to make it big on the stage. Inspired by the experience as an
actor he acquired at this time, he wrote *The Comedienne* and
Ferments, novels that describe artistic life in the late nineteenth century in detail. Both were well-received by readers
and critics. However, the first undisputed masterpiece by the
future Nobel Prize winner was his novel *The Promised Land*,
which was published only in 1899; it is known also partly
thanks to the Oscar-nominated film adaptation by Andrzej
Wajda. The panorama of the society living in industrial Łódź
(pronounced "woodge") described there made Reymont one
of the greatest masters of the realist novel. *The Promised Land*
is unique in that its protagonist was essentially the city, that
huge, ruthless, and bloodthirsty Moloch belching out smoke
through thousands of factory chimneys known as Łódź.² To
this day, this novel is considered to be one of the greatest
masterpieces of European prose from the late nineteenth
and early twentieth centuries. It has shocked generations of
Polish readers, drawing before them a plastic, detailed, and
honest picture of the painful realities of a ravenous capitalism defined by exploitation, hypocrisy, and immorality. *The
Promised Land* was also Reymont's first work that met with
international acclaim, which quickly resulted in its being
translated into numerous European languages.

The Peasants, perhaps one of the most important epics of
modern European culture, for which the author was awarded
the Nobel Prize in Literature in 1924, was written between 1904
and 1909. This novel, divided into four parts corresponding

---

2   See: M. Popiel, *Oblicza wzniosłości. Estetyka powieści młodo-
polskiej*, Krakow 2003, pp. 119–169.

to the seasons of the year and the related rhythms of the periods of the day, of work and rest, presented the history of the simple inhabitants of Lipce in a way that created a mythical image of human existence in every place and time, as well as the Polish nation in its "primordial" form. Antoni Lange, whom I have already quoted, wrote about this work:

> The peasant means the soil, which means nature, which means the eternal primordiality of man and his primordial childhood. The peasant means the open book of life, far removed from any school, research laboratory, or dusty library. The peasant is the half-conscious but unconquered fundament of national life; he is the preservation of customs, traditions, faith, and rituals. The peasant means harsh and difficult work, closely related to the elementary phenomena of nature: the sun and the rain, pleasant and harsh weather, and the perpetually turning wheel of the four seasons of the year. The peasant does obstinate and fierce, but grateful and beloved work in a solemn and ceremonial way.[3]

Reymont's later work was very diverse in regard to subject matter and adopted literary forms. In 1911, he wrote the first mature Polish horror novel, *The Vampire*, which documents the fascination with spiritualist and occult practices that were popular in the early twentieth century, particularly in London. Finally, I should mention 1924's *The Revolt*, an allegorical novel about a revolution by a group of livestock at a farm. Although it has never been translated into English, *The Revolt* bears a striking resemblance to George Orwell's *Animal Farm*, which would be published nineteen years later.

Reymont died on December 5, 1925, in Warsaw.

---

3 A. Lange, *Pochodnie w mroku*, as noted above, pp. 50–51.

A PILGRIMAGE TO JASNA GÓRA

A Pilgrimage to Jasna Góra is one of Reymont's earliest works; in fact, it was his first book. The publication of this literary reportage was all the more important as it ended Reymont's twelve-year losing streak; at the beginning of his literary career, many publishers had turned down his work, and he himself wrote: "Will I ever be published?"[4] So, it was *A Pilgrimage to Jasna Góra* that inaugurated the publishing activity of this promising young author.

This work was the literary aftermath of a pilgrimage in which Reymont participated in 1894 upon the urging of Aleksander Świętochowski, one of the most important Polish essayists of the nineteenth century. In order to gain a more complete context, it is worth recalling that this pilgrimage was not solely a religious event; it was also a camouflaged patriotic demonstration whose aim was to mark the centenary of the Polish national insurrection against Russia and Prussia, widely known as the Kosciuszko Uprising (Reymont wrote a trilogy devoted to this struggle towards the end of his life; it was a titled *1794*). The goal of this journey was also significant. The history of the Marian shrine at Jasna Góra ("Bright Mountain") in Czestochowa reaches back to the fourteenth century, when the Order of Saint Paul the First Hermit, commonly known as the Pauline friars, was brought to Poland from Hungary. However, it was the Polish-Swedish wars of the seventeenth century, colloquially known as the Deluge, that revealed the importance of this place to the Polish nation. This was related to the Swedish army's invasion of the Polish-Lithuanian Commonwealth, which culminated in the Siege of Jasna Góra in 1655. In the collective Polish memory, the victory over the Swedes has been remembered not only as the consolidation of the entire society, but also, and perhaps above all, as possible thanks to

---

4 This comes from an entry in the young Reymont's diary dated May 7, 1892. In: J. Rurawski, *Władysław Reymont*, Warsaw 1988, p. 58.

the aid of Mary, the benefactor who is "terrible as an army set in array" (Song of Songs 6:4). In the nineteenth and early twentieth centuries, Jasna Góra, which was under Russian occupation, was the destination of frequent pilgrimages, even becoming "the spiritual capital of Poland."[5] From then on, it began to play the role of the heart of the nation, a place of memory and hope for the restoration of freedom.[6]

The experiences and reflections narrated by Reymont about his personal experience of the pilgrimage were published in 1895, the same year as two other works very important to Polish culture: Henryk Sienkiewicz's *Quo Vadis* and Stefan Żeromski's *Ravens and Crows Will Peck Us to Pieces*. The very first readers of *A Pilgrimage* made note of the young writer's unique gift of observation.[7] Indeed, Reymont's eye was very perceptive and sensitive to nuances, while his ear was also fine-tuned, thanks to which he could capture the unique rhythm of dialects and the sound of diverse accents he encountered during the pilgrimage. Additionally, this text betrays Reymont's fine literary skill. In this work, Reymont's command of the Polish language is plastic and musical; it fluently moves between impressionistic descriptions and realistic details.

Critics have always been in agreement that *A Pilgrimage to Jasna Góra* is the first successful attempt at writing a reportage in Polish literature. Thus, this work is also an innovative example of modernist prose, mostly because of the introduction of two equal narrators.[8] The protagonist of *A*

5   J. Skarbek, *W dobie rozbiorów i braku państwowości* [in:] J. Kłoczowski, L. Müllerowa, J. Skarbek, *Zarys dziejów Kościoła katolickiego w Polsce*, Krakow 1986, p. 270.

6   See: M. Chmielewski, *Wielka księga duchowości katolickiej*, Krakow 2015, p. 784.

7   See: A. Hutnikiewicz, *Młoda Polska*, Warsaw 2004, p. 279.

8   See: K. Wyka, *Władysław Stanisław Reymont* [in:] *Obraz literatury polskiej XIX i XX wieku. Literatura okresu Młodej Polski*, volume III, Krakow 1967, p. 55; J. Rurawski, *Władysław Reymont*, as noted above, p. 117.

Pilgrimage is not only Reymont himself, but also the "human cluster" and "simple people" whom the author so frequently and enthusiastically allows to speak. Thanks to this, the narration becomes polyphonic, spread onto many points of view and even several distinct worldviews. This method, which would later reappear in *The Promised Land* and *The Peasants*, is naturally not reduced solely to ordinary experiments in style or the writer showing off his skill, but contains deeper reserves of substance. Apart from being an example of literary reportage, *A Pilgrimage* is also the story of the unifying power of religion. Thus, the narrator has been "multiplied" by the author and written to be shared by the community the author encountered and with which he identified at an existential level, despite keeping at a distance in order to meet the requirements of reporting. Community expressed not only in the contents, but also in the style and form of narration, is the life force of this work. Józef Rurawski writes that "[i]t seems that the subject of this reportage is not so much the pilgrimage itself as an account of the social, emotional, and intellectual encounter of conflicting milieus," those of the simple peasant and the intellectual, respectively, "who are temporarily united by the shared convention of the pilgrimage."⁹ Indeed, *A Pilgrimage to Jasna Góra*, just as *The Peasants* would later do, celebrates the vigor of the nature and strength of the group that unites in one spirit and one faith.

The publication of Reymont's *A Pilgrimage to Jasna Góra* in the late nineteenth century, at a period known for good reason as Young Poland, was also of great significance to national culture. One must remember that at this time Poland, which had been occupied and partitioned by Germany, Russia, and Austria, did not appear on official maps of Europe and the world. Furthermore, patriotic activity was harshly punished throughout the entire nineteenth century, while schools put great effort into eradicating any

9 J. Rurawski, *Władysław Reymont*, as noted above, pp. 118–118.

awareness of Polish culture, tradition, or even language from young people who were just entering adulthood. Meanwhile, the Young Poland period, or a Polish form of modernism, entailed a kind of rebirth of national thinking. This was a rebirth not only of national thought, but of art more generally, which, particularly in the late nineteenth century, was considered to be the gauge of identity and spirit. "The patriotic imperative," Andrzej Z. Makowiecki writes, "was to struggle for the continuation of social and national integration in the sphere of culture, counteracting the pressures of the occupier, and advise society on how it should preserve its state of spiritual independence under conditions of slavery."[10] In this context, *A Pilgrimage to Jasna Góra* appears as a patriotic work. Indeed, Reymont presents the beauty of the Polish landscape; the richness of local customs and traditions, dialects and memories; a snippet of the social panorama of "the people of the soil"; and the common experience of dispersed people who were gradually uprooted, this time striving towards the one common destination of the pilgrimage. Thus, Reymont unveils before the reader the image of recovered "social and national integration" under the sign of Jasna Góra, a distinct symbol of the passing down of faith and Polish history.

THE POLISH CULTURE OF PILGRIMAGES

Beginning in late antiquity, pilgrimages have been an expression of piety that involves not only the spirit, but also the body. They were intended to be a depiction of man's temporal way to God. According to the New Testament, "while we are at home in the body we are away from the Lord" (2 Corinthians 5:6). In this way, the pilgrimage becomes a kind of "incarnation of the faith" that imagines the entirety of human life that has been extended to the point of leaving one's earthly home. As God said to Abraham: "Go forth

---

10   A. Z. Makowiecki, *Młoda Polska*, Warsaw 1987, p. 15.

from your land, your relatives, and from your father's house to a land that I will show you" (Genesis 12:1), in order to patiently overcome all discomfort and ultimately arrive at our eternal home in heaven. Every participant of this journey was the manifestation of the apostolic admonition: "You need endurance to do the will of God and receive what he has promised," because "we are not among those who draw back and perish, but among those who have faith and will possess life" (Hebrews 10:39). Finally, in the Christian tradition pilgrimage was supposed to be an opportunity to visit a particular shrine as an earthly, tangible representation of "God's rest" (see Hebrews 4:1), or a place of eternal joy at which one arrives only "through faith and patience" (Hebrews 6:12). This entire theological basis makes the pilgrimage not only evidence of strong persistence in the faith and of entrusting everything to God, but also a unique kind of spiritual exercise intended to strengthen the spirit, which, according to Sacred Scripture, is "tested by fire" (1 Peter 1:7).

Jan Skarbek, an illustrious historian of the Church, has noted that there was an increase in piety, especially in relation to liturgical and para-liturgical encounters, such as the rosary or adoration of the Blessed Sacrament, in the Polish lands in the latter half of the nineteenth century. In that age of Positivism, an era known for the dominant materialist worldview of the intellectual elites, religious practices prescribed by the Church became increasingly common.[11] As Skarbek writes, "the belles lettres are a valuable testament in this case, as religious and moral-ethical themes were widespread there, regardless of whether the author was an orthodox Catholic or not."[12] Important topics relating to the Catholic faith even appeared in the work of Bolesław Prus or Eliza Orzeszkowa, leading Polish authors of the time who rejected God and prayer in their private lives. This phenomenon should not

11   Zob. J. Skarbek, *W dobie rozbiorów*, as noted above, p. 270.
12   Ibid., p. 274.

be surprising. When Poland was partitioned, the Catholic Church was the only area where a dispersed society could become integrated. The world of traditional devotion was not only a window to God, but also a kind of deposit of memory and national identity. Thus, not only deeply religious writers, but also those who had doubts but sincerely sought the truth, as well as those who lacked faith, gravitated towards the Church. This was related to the growing feeling of responsibility for society among the intelligentsia, whose representatives were thus motivated to participate in pilgrimages regardless of their individual levels of religiosity. Although this phenomenon was evident in the Positivist period, it became stronger during the Young Poland era, a cultural movement in which the rebirth of fascination with spiritual life was as strong as the interest in national matters. Here, it is worth quoting the musings of Zdzisław Dębicki, a patriotic poet and thinker from the Young Poland movement:

> During the years of slavery, national feeling became so unified with religious feeling that there was a phenomenon of religious patriotism in Poland, something unknown elsewhere. All our national liberation movements were deeply religious in nature.... It is a fact that 'national Catholicism' participated in all our struggles for independence and became very closely caught up with the traditions of these struggles.... The association of religion with nationality became so powerful in Poland that wherever the Catholic Church fought for its rights in the territory of the former Polish-Lithuanian Commonwealth, the struggle for Polishness to be given the right to exist closely followed.... Let us now go to a village parish, to its simple, often wooden and modest walls on which kitschy paintings hang; it is tied by a thousand mysterious threads to our soul, our

memory, and the tradition living within us that time has failed to obliterate.[13]

Pilgrimages have a major and permanent place in the traditions of Polish Catholicism. Their public nature unquestionably influenced this. The uniquely Polish style of piety has always been marked by attachment to the "tangible" dimension of faith, a love for its external, sometimes greatly diversified manifestation, and clear, unabashed, collective identification with the Catholic Church. Naturally, such aspirations were favorable to the development of diverse forms of prayer, which over the course of time became richer and more sophisticated. "The characteristic trait of Polish religiosity," Skarbek writes, "is its massive nature and its predilection for exalted ceremonies with elaborate rituals."[14] Furthermore, many Poles took part in pilgrimages, especially to Jasna Góra, in the late nineteenth and early twentieth centuries. In Reymont's time, there were approximately 1,000 pilgrimages with 400,000 participants going to the shrine each year. At that time, the major solemnities attracted up to 100,000 believers.[15] This occurred in defiance of the efforts of the partitioning powers, which intended to weaken public manifestations of religious devotion. The more aggressive the external oppression, the stronger the Polish nation's need for engaged forms of religious practice.

MICHAŁ GOŁĘBIOWSKI is a historian of literature, essayist, and writer who deals with the theological bases of classical literature. He has published the book *Niewiasta z perłą. Szkice o*

13   Z. Dębicki, *Podstawy kultury narodowej*, Warszawa 1927, pp. 46–53.
14   Zob. J. Skarbek, *W dobie rozbiorów*, as noted above, p. 270.
15   Zob. M. Chmielewski, *Wielka księga duchowości katolickiej*, as noted above, p. 784.

Maryi Pannie w świetle duchowości katolickiej ("Lady with the Pearl: Sketches on Mary in Light of Catholic Spirituality"), while his collection of essays *Bezkres poranka. O teologii poetyckiej i teologiach kontrkultury* ("The Infinitude of the Morning: On Poetic Theology and the Theologies of Counterculture") will be published in the coming months. Currently, he is completing his PhD in Polish literature at the Jagiellonian University in Krakow, Poland.

Feeling and faith speak to me more strongly
Than a wise man's looking glass and eye.
— *Adam Mickiewicz*

The Church at Praga

MAY 5, 1894

I WENT EQUIPPED WITH AS LITTLE AS POS-
sible: my long boots, an old coat, flat hat, and umbrella
did not distinguish me much from the crowds gathered
on the squares and road in front of the church. Besides,
nobody paid much attention to me; everyone was absorbed
in their preparations for the journey and instead looked
at the cloudy horizon. There was a little bit of rain, but I
could not see much concern in their faces. The whole place
was swarming. I pushed through with difficulty to get to
the cemetery and was pleased to see no veils, overcoats, or
fedoras. These were ordinary folk. Their faces were simple,
scorched from heat, and hardened, and their clothes were
gray. I saw in the eyes of this crowd that their souls were
overcome with a feeling I could not understand. I mingled
with them, taking in hundreds of conversations and count-
less faces. The greyness of their ordinariness and their marketplace babble bored and dismayed me. I felt completely
alien and alone in this crowd. I would have liked to fall
into this human wave to sense the current that must have
been flowing over them, but I could not. As I stood there,
a square-faced peasant clad in a gray coat with a rosary
around his neck approached me.

"Are you going, too?" he asked.

"I am. We are going together."

"So, you are going with us?"

I replied in the affirmative and tried to have a chat with
him, but the peasant grew silent and walked away. Once
again, I stood and did not know what to do. There was no
chance I could get inside the church, as the path to it had

been barricaded with people. I could only hear singing and an organ playing as well as isolated words from the homily; convulsive and brief waves of tears fluttered like the wind. The priest was talking to those who were about to leave. All were kneeling and had taken off their head coverings; they passively, submissively, and attentively listened to him.

The gray sky continued to sow a little rain and threaten with the prospect of a downpour; above all, I was worried that I was no longer listening but instead stared with little joy at the blossoming lilacs and the reddish, youthful greenery of the chestnut trees. Finally, it became completely quiet and this thousand-strong crowd began to slowly drift away in thin streams.

As we walked half-asleep, passing a bridge, a green park, and the city skyline spread out on the opposite side of the Vistula, these gray, diminutive, and harsh silhouettes of people with their sharp profiles, rough and thick faces, square figures slightly bent over while carrying their baggage, and with rosaries hanging around their necks, moved; they had an enormous power and a sense of having been anointed.

A bronze cross covered with garlands of paper roses swayed at the beginning of the procession amidst a cloudy, rainy aura. The bustle of the street came in a tumultuous wave; the bells of streetcars rang one after the other; the rattle of cars sounded deaf; factory chimneys scattered shreds of fog over the city; and at the bottom the grayish-yellow depths of the river splashed against the bridgehead. Everywhere, the hurried, active, and constrained life of the city bubbled; it was marked by the struggle for existence and for amusement.

When I compiled all this in my mind, I saw a caravan drawn by one horse with a blue coffin at the fore protruding from the bridge. One single woman was behind it; she was holding her dress with her hand and walked in an automatic way with her head held down... I then caught glimpses of her dry profile, which had been eroded away by pain.

Despite this, I still saw that raw image of a clenched mouth; the redness of her swollen, teary pupils; and that whole expression of seemingly petrified pain.

I felt a certain dark and inexplicable anxiety of internal weariness, but when I looked at those onlookers standing on the pavement who were gathered in packs and gave us stupid and ironic looks and at that disgusting rabble that mocked those who were going, I felt a great desire to slap them, but I had to restrain myself somehow. I counted the windows and streetlights, and I was even able to gaze at the architecture of the new Warsaw homes for five minutes and try to count how many revolutions the carriage made; I would have done anything to not see that huddled urban mob.

When I walked past the turnpikes, I departed Warsaw with one frank word: "Finally!" At least for ten days, in any case....

2

Ochota

THIS TOWN CONSISTED OF A DOZEN OR SO dirty and really shabby houses; it seemed as if someone had put great effort in creating something that was ugly to the point of repulsion. All the pilgrims gathered there and joined together in one company. We had waited for an hour or so before they all arrived. There were seventy-six carriages carrying people and their belongings. My carriage driver, who even committed himself to driving me to my destination for ten rubles,[1] carried numerous bundles. The pilgrims paid thirty, or at most fifty kopecks for the whole journey. I paid a membership fee, because I had learned that I could travel with my belongings for three rubles. The carriages formed a long line at the side of the road, and the people lay down wherever they could next to the cross. The tavern was overflowing, but its owner was in a bad mood.

"What a crowd! The people here are packed like herrings in a barrel!" I said to kill time.

"My dear sir, this is a company from Praga. They are all a bunch of yokels, rabble that drinks tea!"

"Would you prefer a group from Warsaw?"

"Would I! My dear sir, over the course of one hour they would empty fifty casks of beer and a million bottles of vodka!" he yelled ecstatically as his cheeks grew red with warm nostalgia.

---

1   In 1772, 1773, and 1795, Poland was partitioned between Russia, Prussia, and Austria, disappearing from the map of Europe. Following the Congress of Vienna, a semi-autonomous Kingdom of Poland under Russian control was established. In the Kingdom of Poland, also known as Congress Poland, two currencies simultaneously functioned: the ruble (one hundred kopecks) and the zloty (one hundred groszy).

I had ceased listening to him and walked out because an older "brother," the one who was the pilgrimage's guide, and who had the most authority over the people, was supposed to give a speech by the cross.

I was standing so far from him that I could barely hear what he was saying. I only saw ashen hair, a grayish face, and tragic gesticulation. He must have been speaking loudly and emphatically and reached many hearts, because every so often there was a murmur of sighs; the crowd would swing, someone would moan, and isolated noises would flow. Immediately afterwards, I would again be surrounded by silence, mesmerized by the waves of this human sea....

They formed a huge crowd, amid a landscape of poor houses and weedy, dirty plants; they themselves were poor, hobbled from hard work, tattered like rags by everyday poverty, and barely clothed. The pale sun shone as if it had been poured through a sieve on their uncovered, blond, disheveled, and rarely combed hair, while the cold wind blew from the side and pinched their bare feet with frost. I looked at them and asked myself: who made them leave their homes, families, farms, wages, bowls of potatoes, beds, and quilts and walk dozens of miles eating only dry bread, sleeping in the road, and bearing the untold burden of the nomadic life? What was this force that had carried them away from their nests and thrown them into a diverse crowd, dragging and guiding them?

Before I had been able to answer, the crowd started swinging, got on their feet, and sang loudly: "Who will entrust himself to the Lord!"

And so, we went, truly going along the whitish trail of the road across large fields marked by chimneys. The wind tugged at their hair and blew at the white veil of some "sister," which was supposed to be a flag. A long row of poplar trees with reddish young leaves formed a blackish mass that stretched all the way to Raszyn, whispering with its branches. Birds flew away from us into the field, while frightened skylarks fell like bullets onto the green grass and became silent. It was chilly, the heavens were gray and full; they looked like the snowy mountaintops of piling clouds. It was getting increasingly calm, because we were getting away from the city; only singing disturbed the calm with its broad rhythm, and echoed throughout the green grain crops:

You will sit on a stern lion without fear,
And ride an enormous dragon . . .

Song emanated from all their breasts and all the hearts seemed to place their entire faith in these words, while all the souls began to wobble and flow together in this three hundred-year-old song filled with exceptionally powerful sounds.

This is the cement that binds and unites them, I thought, as I scanned their faces.

I wanted to find some familiar face, but there was none. This general song that was sung together was coming to an end. The older brother was chanting a different one, but at the same time ten different dissonant melodies began to resound. Then I saw that this enormous body did not have one main interior; it had a dozen of them. I could see hundreds of gangs walking together, grouped by parish, village, or even county. Someone always walked at the fore, opened a book, and began to chant a new song. This formed a cacophony, a severe chaos that was impossible to listen to; the lament of these voices created a horribly droning vortex that unmercifully assaulted my ears like some harsh and raspy clatter. I walked half a mile ahead of them and noticed the "sister" with the banner who trotted corpulently, as if she were wearing crackows.[2] I ran up to her and asked her something with my hat in my hand.

---

2 Shoes with very long toes that were popular in the fifteenth century and are also known as poulaines or pikes. Their name refers to the fact that they were believed to have originated in Krakow, Poland.

Saying "sister" in a foot soldier's voice with old-fashioned sweetness made me feel impertinent. I bowed and left, but immediately afterwards some "Praga brother" covered in denim who wielded a suitcase over his shoulder and held a flask for vodka at one side and mug on the other came up to me. He asked me with a voice that had grown hoarse, probably from saying many goodbyes:

"Are you going to Czestochowa, brother?"

"Yes, sir."

"Let's go together."

"But we already are all going together," I replied as I occupied myself with scanning his face, which had become perfectly marked with the traces of friendly conversation.

"You must be from Warsaw, right?"

"Yes, sir, I am from Warsaw."

"Stop with this 'sir' business! We are all brothers and sisters here," he said energetically.

Then, out of the blue, he asked: "What is your profession, brother?"

I pushed back a little, but I somehow ended up answering, while he carefully looked at my jacket, felt the bag at my side, and touched my boots and legs.

"You won't make it to Czestochowa, brother. With legs like that, you can ask someone to carry you from Praga to Warsaw, but to Czestochowa?! Are you carrying a lot of fuel? What about money?"

I quickly gave him a cigar. He bit it with his teeth, lit it, inhaled a ton of smoke into his lungs, exhaled, and said somewhat softly: "This must have cost at least ten kopecks! Oh boy, you must be quite the professional!"

I shifted my anger to the probable disappearance of the fuel and those rubles, so I joined the company. They were going incredibly fast. Some sang, but the rest softly chatted. I heard the most diverse details about farms and villages; it seemed that the price of grain was what interested them the most. I kept hearing the questions: "Where are you from, brother?" and "Where are you from, sister?" everywhere. A drawn-out, singsong accent dominated. Everywhere, I saw hard heads, small foreheads, seemingly wild profiles, and exceedingly bright glances with child-like expressions. They looked at me distrustfully, and when I tried to join their conversations, they grew silent and began to sing.

I left angry at the stupid costume that evidently distinguished me from the rest and the sophistication that had shaped me in such a way that I was incapable of finding simple and natural words and concepts that would allow me access to their souls. I searched for distinct faces and outfits in vain; there was nothing but homespun fabrics whose hue ranged from blood red to flaxen. This sea of male heads and female ones clad in gray, red, yellow, and crimson scarves created a moving wave of primary colors mixed together. It was only near Raszyn that I noticed three silhouettes that stuck out from the bright background from afar. These were three heads wearing enormous straw hats with white veils tied around them. They were walking together and every now and again they drowned in the thicket of heads; only sometimes could I discern these slender and simple figures, but shortly afterwards a human wave swept over them.

I really wanted to find them, but I could not.

3

Raszyn (Our First Break)

THERE WERE SEVERAL SEVERELY DAMAGED
brick houses, a church, and an enormous tavern in this
town. On the left was a park consisting of a mass of trees
and ponds that looked like blue mirrors. That was the whole
town. Because of our numbers, the church had become so
crowded that I did not even bother to try to go inside and
have a look. Three-quarters of our company lay down in
front of the tavern and on the road to graze. The tavern
was crowded, and right before the entrance I saw the following scene:

One of the brothers was leaning against the table. His
red eyes stared at the ceiling, and he stood next to another
brother, an old peasant with curly hair and facial features
that looked as if they had been sculpted by a saw. A green
wool belt was tied around his reddish outer garment. He
wore leather riding boots and a brass rosary was draped
around his neck, and he had a holy card in his hand. He was
blowing on the eyes of a seated person; touching his fingers;
making hypnotizing gestures over his face and across his
eyes; spitting on them and rubbing the spit; and brushing
him with the card. Next, he placed two saliva-covered straws
and the card on a shell and lit them on fire. He blew the
smoke over these sick eyes and half-whispered some curses
and prayers of healing. By the time he was finished with
the ceremony, he stepped back a little and said with great
certainty, as if he were anointing him:

"You, brother, must believe that God's word, my word,
and my desire will help you; yes, they will. The Lord Jesus
told Peter: 'Come to me upon these waters.' Peter could not
make up his mind and thought that he could not stay on
the water, and so he sank to the ground right away. Then,

Jesus grabbed him by the hair and said: 'If you had trusted in me, Peter, that you could walk on water, you would have crossed the lake.' Therefore, you, brother, must pray and believe that you will be healthy through the graces of the Holy Lady of Czestochowa. And you will be healthy again. We can do what we can do, but God will do the rest. Amen!" The rest of those who had gathered looked on, piously concentrating on what was going on, beat their breasts, and loudly repeated:

"God will help with the rest. Amen!"

Solemn faith was evident in their faces. They believed so strongly in these words and their great souls submitted to this force that I got some kind of uncertain goose bumps. My brain, meanwhile, started to think about images from distant times and lands where Christ walked across sorry, burnt soil and where throngs of the poor awaited him. He touched the eyes of the blind who then began to see; He told the dead to arise, and they were resurrected, while those aching, tormented souls clung to his feet like spikes and sang: "Hosanna! Hosanna!" However, Jesus left as sad as he had been when he had arrived and gave blessings, whispering: "As long as you have the light, believe in the light."

A crowd had gathered on the square in front of the church, getting to leave.

I saw those three heads amidst the carriages, but by the time I had arrived, they once again got lost in the crowd.

We left a little bit later.

The singing sounded the same, but it resounded in a somewhat more energetic way. A long caravan stood at the end of the procession. We walked across a smooth and well-kept road. There were black rows of trees far away. There were many statues and crosses everywhere, and the elder brother stopped in front of each one, after which a deaf moment of silence followed until all the heads bowed, all the knees bent, and all the breasts bellowed out songs of praise that scattered across the fields.

By the time we stopped for the night, I already had begun to feel a kind of sluggishness, just as the red sun sluggishly descended behind the forest....

4

Łazy

THE MASS OF PEOPLE LITERALLY FLOODED the village. There was not a single house, barn, or backyard where dozens of people had not crowded. They bandaged their legs, made tea, shared their provisions with one another, and talked freely. Everyone crowded into the buildings and under their roofs. This was a veritable small town fair with all its hubbub. I could tell that the village was near Warsaw, because as I could not find lodging anywhere, I wandered from house to house and noticed that every home was exceptionally clean and orderly. Almost every home had a decent, whitewashed room. Everywhere, tables were covered with tablecloths and plates were kept in cabinets. There were fine images of the saints on the walls; beds were neatly made and covered with bedspreads; the ceilings and roof beams were fully decorated with ribbons and a rainbow of colorful papers. It was very cold, and I was getting hungry.

After much effort, I was finally able to get inside a house, where I drank hot water mixed with milk.

I sat in the sand by the road because it was slightly warmer and enjoyed my milk, while dusk spread across the green fields and stifled everything. The black wall of forest standing next to the road grew darker and seemed to undress. The contours of trees, villages, and distant hills seemed to disperse and merge with navy blue shadows. An increasingly profound silence was falling; the only occasional sounds were horses neighing and snorting, some individual voices speaking, the last verse of a pious song bellowing out from one of the barns, and the choral croaking of frogs in the meadows.

The fog was slowly giving way to cold grayness and morose spaces.

The subdued, sleepy half-whispers of prayers wandered between the houses like fading flickers, like the fires that were going out in these same houses, until everything scattered, grew quiet, and melted into nighttime rest.

The light had not gone out in my hosts' house yet. I went inside to get a little bit warmer. A dozen or so sisters were so packed on the straw that it was impossible to toss and turn; they were already asleep.

These people from Warsaw's rural vicinity were very talkative; they incessantly inundated me with questions like:

"Are you with your family?"

"No, I'm here by myself."

"So, you're not here with your wife?"

"That's correct."

"So, your woman let you go by yourself?"

"I don't have a wife."

"What?!" the host asked incredulously.

"It's true; I'm not married."

"But you're from Warsaw?"

"Yes."

"The men there have it bad; their wives don't let them have any freedom."

There was a moment of silence, after which they tried to outdo one another with telling me about their troubles and problems.

Finally, the hostess offered me coffee. I declined, asking for more milk and dark bread instead.

"You see, my dear? Sir, my man got so spoiled in Warsaw that he won't even touch dark bread. I have to buy him rye bread all the time, and he won't go anywhere near milk."

"I've had it up to here with delicacies like milk and rye bread."

They kept talking and talking while I was overcome with sleepiness, so I went to the barn to sleep.

I found a couple square inches of space that had not been taken, turned on my side, and I do not even know when I had fallen asleep.

I was sleeping like a baby when someone began to shake me and yell:

"Brother, you have to get up."

This was the sister sleeping next to me who had just woken up.

I shut my eyes and got back to sleep. Lord, would I have liked to sleep longer! However, the frosty cold penetrated me, bells were violently ringing, and streaks of light were creeping in through the barn's large doors. The clatter of people getting up and the awareness of the fact that I had to get up, too, stopped me from falling asleep. I got up, and although I shivered from the cold, I went across the meadow to the other side of the road and performed my ablution under bright-green willow trees in a dark-blue orchard. The water was so icy that it almost burned me, but it was very refreshing nonetheless.

The world was still dark.

In the east, the pinkish-gold dawn was merely sprinkled on the darkness, while trees, the grass, and wheat stood in drowsy silence, soaked with dew and resounding with life. The air was fresh and robust. The forest was almost black with damp green and darkness; only the slenderest peaks were outlined, like lace on a pearly morning. A broad gust of melted opal, the wave of dawn filled with charm and power spread across the fields; it was like the damp and aromatic breath of the awakening earth. Meanwhile, the crowing of roosters was coming from the households in the village.

New sounds — babbling, neighing, the rattling of carriages on their way, and prayers said out loud — slowly fused with this morning silence.

We gathered by the cross. Their faces were drowsy and blue from the cold and their clothes were crumpled, but their eyes shone brightly. A proud peasant with a monk's cap on his head and sharp ascetic facial features covered by a wreath of fresh greenery raised the cross. He rang a bell and intoned in his low voice:

> *With the morning radiance breaking*
> *Earth in all her glory waking*

Then the simple people in the crowd joined the song with their hearts and sang it in exaltation with an overwhelmingly powerful voice:

> *Sky and sea, Thine own creation*
> *Hymn Thee, Lord, in adoration*

Their voices flowed in a large wave towards that morning's radiance that by then had covered half the horizon; they fell like a cascade on the ground, resounded over the houses, permeated the fields of ground, sprayed onto the opal space, and resounded in the forest echoes and the flowers in the orchards. Bolstered by the voices of nature, they rose up in a powerful hymn and spoke of the Lord's benevolence and glory. Freed of everything that is dirty, poor, and transient, their hearts rose above the world. This was a mighty song, one whose beauty, which I had never experienced before, was powerful. Only amid these wonders of the spring that surrounded us, and that they sang about, did it exert an unheard-of charm.

The sun had risen, making everything gold and crimson. We were walking fast, but I wanted to lie down somewhere in a furrow amid this swaying rye and look into the blue, listen to the skylarks singing and the murmur of the trees, and melt into this powerful song that resounded like a bugle of joy. My breast inhaled the spring, while my eyes wandered dreamily. . . . We passed forests that bubbled with the chirping of birds. There were fields as far as the eye could see; they were deliciously arable and green. We walked across villages filled with apple trees covered in pink buds and pears sprinkled with flowers that looked like snow. We walked for eleven versts[1] without taking a break, but without a trace of exhaustion.

1   An obsolete unit of measurement used in nineteenth-century Russia equivalent to about 0.6629 miles or 1.0668 kilometers.

5

A Settlement in Tarczyn

THIS WAS A QUADRILATERAL AREA CON-
sisting mostly of brick houses. I could still feel the nearby
presence of Warsaw. According to a sign in the market
square, this town had seventy-four houses, while some local
cicerone informed me that in addition to numerous public
institutions, Tarczyn also boasted of twenty-four pubs. In
other words, there was one pub for every three houses, an
adequate number. The heavy façade of a church built in
some style-less style peered over the road. A stone statue
of Christ stood in a side wing that served as something
akin to a vestibule. Over the large altar, a colorful, round
window projected a cloud of colorful light. In any case, it
was nothing worth seeing. Our break was to last several
hours, so I went to look for something to eat.

"Brother," a sister who was so veiled that I did not even
see any part of her face whispered to me, "you wouldn't
happen to know if all the carriages have arrived? I can't
seem to find mine."

I asked her about the carriage driver and the horse.

"He is a tall man with brown hair, and his carriage was
pulled by a couple horses."

We went to look for them. We finally found them, but
it was clear that the driver was neither tall nor had brown
hair, nor did he have a couple of horses.

The market square was filled with benches and long
tables on which tin samovars,[1] steaming pots, and piles of
loaves of bread and rolls had been placed.

---

1 A now largely obsolete metal device used to boil water for tea
originating in Russia, but whose popularity spread to the Middle
East and Central Asia.

"My dear pious brothers and sisters! Come and buy tea; two groszy for tea without sugar and four for tea with sugar. Come, pious people, and get fresh borscht and hot cabbage soup!" the merchants called.

I sat next to the well to eat hot borscht with sausage and potatoes. Even though its flavor had a hint of old galosh, I really enjoyed it tremendously. I paid sixteen groszy for this breakfast. A sister sat next to me and drank tea. She coughed up six groszy from her handkerchief, banged the money against the table, and started bartering like there was no tomorrow.

"Four groszy for a glass of tea! I'll be darned! What do you need all that money for? A little bit of water and a pinch of sugar, and you want four groszy. In Warsaw, we paid five groszy, but it was good tea; it was black and sweet."

"You're going to get an indulgence, but you are bartering as if you were at a bazaar," the merchant said.

"An indulgence is an indulgence, but a rip-off is a rip-off. You're squabbling like Jews!" she yelled loudly, although she paid and left.

A whole cluster of rural sisters, most of whom were young and ugly, arrived. They sat by the well, unpacked their bundles, and took out some bread. Some ate, while others washed and combed their hair, something akin to their morning bath. One veiled sister sitting across from me turned red with anger and hissed:

"How crass they are, undressing in the middle of the market square!" she said as she spat with disgust.

"If you are such a lady, then why are you going on a pilgrimage with simpletons? You should wait for the aristocratic company," an older sister said calmly.

"Everyone knows that we are peasants, but only some know what you are," someone else added, this time harshly and with a sense of derision.

I left because I felt embarrassed by that veiled woman.

I saw those three mysterious veiled women I had spotted before; some older woman with very noble and sad facial features and a boy who looked like he was about ten accompanied them.

Women encircled them and yelled with admiration:

"So, this child is offering himself up and going to Czestochowa by foot!"

They blessed him out loud:

"Dear child, may you grow so that the Holy Virgin gives you all that is the best when you come to her, my sweet boy!"

I wanted to get a closer look at these sisters through their veils, but they stopped me:

"My dear brother!"

I turned around and noticed a face that was young but somehow black and emaciated; it had been gnawed at by some kind of suffering, and all that was left were facial features and an expression of hopeless withdrawal in her big, bright eyes.

"Are you going to Czestochowa with us, brother?" she asked. I listened to her singsong voice with delight and saw that she chewed dry black bread with difficulty.

"Yes. Are you sick, sister?" I asked, noticing that she barely moved.

"It's nothing. The Virgin Mary will heal me. I have offered up my suffering to her and have been walking since Łomża. My dear brother, I have stopped you so that you could help me. In Praga, bad people stole fifteen rubles from me. The evil one is outwitting me. I did nothing, I didn't even curse; I prayed and I'm going. Good people help me. Please, brother; I haven't the audacity to ask these simpletons. I can humble myself in front of the Blessed Virgin, but it's no honor to do so in front of simpletons."

I gave her what I could, because I was convinced that she really was in need.

By this time, I was pretty good at distinguishing the petty nobility from the peasants and from that handful of people from Praga. The peasants always walked together, chaotically stretching out in the scorching sun; their facial features were thick, but less tired. Meanwhile, the nobility concentrated around the carriages, sat on benches by the tables, sought out shadows, chose better roads, and spoke more softly; they were more discrete in various functions and their introverted, predominantly regular faces had a kind of quietness and dignity.

They raised their heads higher and had a caste-like feeling of superiority.

Those from Praga, meanwhile, looked for pubs.

I recognized their self-contained, restless facial features and arrogant glances. They yelled loudly and tried to be in charge everywhere. It was only that day that I noticed these enormous differences between them and these silent antagonisms at every turn. The peasants and especially the city slickers made fun of their aristocratic brothers.

Oh, those city slickers! They were everywhere, knew everything, knew how to deal with everything, and always looked for opportunities to make money. All their carriages belonged to them. They came from Stanisławów, Radzymin, and Nowo-Mińsk. They traveled mostly to make money. There were those who went to Czestochowa four times each summer and made between thirty and fifty rubles every time.

As I was writing these words, I was sitting in a carriage as two Jews came up to me and calmly studied my shoes. I was curious what would happen until one of them said:

"Dear sir, you won't make it to Czestochowa. You need new soles. We can make you new ones in one hour for just one ruble." Right then he started to take off my shoe.

"Get lost!" I sweetly replied to his thoughtfulness.

"Oy, vey! What a nasty way of talking. I sincerely want you to make it to the Virgin Mary, but you won't make it there like this because of your soles. What is this? This is just paper, damp tissue paper! Do you, dear sir, think that this is a walk in the Saxon Garden?"

I did not answer, and he finished angrily:

"You don't want new soles? In that case, you will walk to Czestochowa carrying your shoes rather than wearing them." And he left.

The sun started to get hotter and hotter, and it was getting unbearable. I looked for refuge in a pub and took a nap. At two-thirty, we went to Grójec, some twelve and a half versts away. The sun was scorching hot, and the road was so dusty that after a few minutes my mouth was filled with dust. For a moment, I stood near the end of the procession so that I could look at the carriages. The area we walked across was filled with wavy hills, good soil, and beautiful greenery all around. The specks of whiteness in the villages consisted of walls that had become covered with grain and orchards.

A dozen or so old women who lacked the strength to walk were sitting in the carriages, as were sick people who had embarked in order to ask for healing. The sisters greeted me with God's Word and chatted gaily. One of them in particular attracted my attention. She was very old; she turned her incredibly wrinkled and transparent face, which was as lucid as wax, towards me.

"Are you with us, brother?" she asked as she drilled me with her wonderfully violet eyes.

"Yes. You cannot walk, sister?" I asked.

"I haven't been able to walk for twenty years. That was Jesus' will, so what can I do? Before I die, I want to see the Blessed Virgin and ask her for a light and speedy death."

Tears glazed her eyes.

"Why do you want a speedy death?"

"It's already my time, brother. I've been alive for 102 years. My birthday was on the Feast of the Presentation. You want me to live longer, brother, but I miss my people."

"Are you alone, sister? Have you no children?"

"I did have children, brother, eight of them in all. My boys were as healthy and strong like horses, while no lord's daughters were prettier than mine. All have passed away and now I am alone like an old hen. Man, pestilence, and God took away all my chicks. I've been an orphan for twenty years. I have no grandchildren, nor any family, and I'm all alone. What am I to do in this world?"

She looked at the vast terrain of fields where young ears of grain bowed, at the cherry trees by the road whose last flowers the wind had sprinkled on her silver hair, and at the azure sky. She became absorbed in listening to the song of the brothers who walked before us, these faded tones that poured into the world like an increasingly transparent stream. I did not dare to interrupt her pensiveness, because it seemed to me that she was seeing all her relatives, that she was talking to specters and blessing everything with her dying being.

"It's beautiful in these parts, brother. The people are faithful, and the soil is golden. I haven't been to Czestochowa yet. Although I'm a cripple, for five years I scrimped and saved all I could so that I could go to the Blessed Virgin. Our Blessed Lady has allowed me to live to this day, and even helped me to buy some beads. I paid a hundred zlotys for this necklace."

She spoke for a long time, but I kept silent, because I had entered a dreamy state as I was moved by the tragic melancholy of a life so long and lonely, her faith, and her indefatigable strength that could be shattered by neither people nor time.

"I yearn for those I loved. People respect and honor me, but to them I'm like a mute, because I'm the last of a world that has been long dead, the very last indeed. It's time for me to die, brother."

Once again, she fell into an old woman's rumination as her venerable head, covered with a prolific mane of hair, rested on her breast. She shut her violet eyes and began to nap.

I walked away from her so I would not disturb her and quickly lost myself in the crowd.

It was still scorching hot, so sweat streamed down the faces and necks of our brothers, while their eyes shone with the fever of exhaustion. The road sloped upward up to Głuchów, a very pretty estate. At that point, it turned into a ditch and began to descend. I walked a trail that ran across the peak of the trench that was guarded by a huge privet hedge plant. Just then, a violent, brief scream flashed like a thunderbolt and the whole polychromatic crowd that was walking downhill literally snapped into two halves, while between them a black horse hitched to a long wagon bolted uphill.

One little boy tried with all his might to stop it, but the animal was mad and ran into the crowd and trampled people with the rabid force that is unleashed when an animal is spooked. Neither a thunderbolt nor a tempest could break trees with the force of the fear that had scattered those people. A chaotic mess consisting of bowed heads, faces that had grown blue with sudden fear, and bodies falling onto the ground to avoid the horse and rolling into the ditch and running for the fields appeared. I could only hear one moan, similar to a roar, while the black beast ran above this quivering, scrunched, tangled mass of flattened bodies. This was a poignantly powerful image.

The horse was stopped only after it had passed the crowd of pilgrims and trampled four women.

This was a fortunate outcome, because their number could have just as easily been four hundred.

The wounded were taken onto the wagon and carried off to Grójec to see a doctor. There were sobs everywhere; a shadow of sorrow frightened all souls and struck them with grief. When we resumed our journey, our songs no longer resounded so gaily; tears and woe were discernible in our voices.

As soon as I had noticed the church in Grójec, I passed everyone. It was very small. As I walked up the hill on whose peak the church rested, I noticed the three veiled women against the backdrop of an old wooden bell tower;

apparently, they had arrived even faster than I. There were many locals awaiting us in the cemetery and adjacent square.

Inside the church, a benevolent chill and darkness wrapped around me, but I did not have time to see anything; our company was arriving quickly. An older brother walked with a cross at the front of the crowd; behind him a compact group of those who could fit inside the church walked forcefully. They walked through the church in silence and with such strength and such a harsh, oblivious expression of spontaneous power that I fearfully stepped aside.

The older brother rested the cross against the altar and the entire forest of people fell onto the ground with a silent thump. Dust rose from the ground and like a gold fog hidden in the streaks of sunlight, covering everyone like a cloud. A second dust, that of whispered prayers, soared to the roof of the church.

6

Grójec

THIS TOWN WAS A VERY DECENT COUNTY
seat. Its only flaw was that its cobblestone was so sharp that
I could barely walk on it. I found a pastry shop, but it did
not serve tea.

"We do have beer, though," the owner suggested.

I was so incredibly thirsty that I would have agreed to
a drink of sulfuric acid.

That was the first time I saw a newspaper since I had left
Warsaw, but I decided to give it a rest; the screaming of the
blackbirds was so terrifying that I had to get out quickly.

After an hour-long break, we went on. We had to walk
seven versts to the place where we would spend the night.
The evening sky grew reddish while blue wrapped along the
more distant landscapes. I began to feel even more tired;
my legs started to get tangled and my sensitivity to certain
things became heightened. Because I had to walk the whole
way without any head covering and my umbrella not only
did not fully protect me against the sun, but also could not
be used everywhere, my head hurt.

7

Belsk

I WAS HAPPY TO HEAR THAT WE WOULD BE
spending the night in Bielsk, because I was running out of
energy. Some sister who was overcome with mercy told me
that she had reserved lodging for me and several other "delicate persons" at the sexton's residence. I happily agreed and
went to the church. Enormous chestnut trees sprinkled with
flowers surrounded the church like a wreath and wrapped
their green shoulders around its slender and pretty body.
Because I did not have the strength to push inside, I sat in
the middle of a sandy road across from the church doors
in order to listen to the May devotion.

I saw a painting of the Assumption of the Virgin Mary
behind the altar. Directly in front of it were green geranium
leaves and red flowers covering the picture frame. Bouquets
of lilacs and daffodils glimmered between the candlesticks.
The Virgin Mary's bright face steeped in awe emerged from
this aromatic shield: she had such sweetness in her raised
eyes while her open mouth breathed such goodness that
looking at this bright and pure figure gave me great joy. An
organ resounded with the subdued melody of a litany, while
the candles' golden flames grew even brighter, for dusk was
falling slowly and pouring into the pink glow of the sunset.
The people filled up all the empty space, kneeling in the
middle of the road, in the garden, across from the church,
and under the blossoming apple trees.

Nightingales hidden in the orchards began their songs
of night and love; they poured out chattering cascades with
unspeakably soft tones, while the organ sounded with a
quiet, ceremonious psalmody and the people sang in full
voice amidst the silence of the coming night, brightened by
the halo of violet reflections created by the copper afterglow.

I wanted nothing more than to have enough feeling to be able to embrace and absorb the beauty of everything I saw and heard then! It seemed as if my soul had raised itself up from its weariness and its wings spread thanks to the rhythms of these songs, this playing, the singing of the nightingale, and the aromas and colors; my soul expanded infinitely and drank bliss and oblivion from this well of beauty. All the faces grew bright and all the eyes, focused the Virgin's holy face, sowed brilliance, while all hearts sang in harmony in these dark depths filled with the golden dust of light. I felt as if I were becoming part of the crowd kneeling next to me and swimming the same current as they in the song whose conclusion resounded:

> *Goodnight, blessed Lady,*
> *Conceived without sin —*
> *Goodnight!*
> *Goodnight, fragrant lily,*
> *Immaculate Mary —*
> *Goodnight!*

The ferment of this song, the cordiality of these sounds, the intoxicating aromas, and all the emotions that pulsated in the crowd struck at my heart, permeating it with ecstasy. I felt new and intense goosebumps. I would kneel on that sand under navy-blue heavens, adorned by the silver of the stars among this songful crowd. I only wanted them to sing more softly: "Goodnight, fragrant lily, Goodnight!" All I wanted was for those mild sounds, those lily rhythms, those lights that were sounds, that harmony of hearts united at the feet of the Immaculate, which seemed to break off from the background and fly off into space with ethereal smile and hang above us in silence, to sway my soul.

I would have liked to kneel like that because it seemed to me that I had forgotten about the sorrows of existence — fragmented, I circled around infinities that were as blue as the robe of the One that had just floated away. I no longer knew anything: I only felt.

It took me a long time to sober up on the dew in a garden.

I went to the presbytery to look at the newspapers. The local parish priest, a certain Father Grabowski, received me very kindheartedly and we enjoyed a nice chat while drinking tea until twelve.

As I walked back, the moon was shining, but there was darkness saturated with stains of light under the chestnut next to the church, while silver glistened from the steeples.

I stumbled upon a body stretched out on the ground near some big trees and heard soft sobs.

The moon rose higher and through its branches placed silver glimmers on her tilted head.

There was deep silence all around. Sleep embraced the earth with its comforting arms; only the sobs of an unfortunate pilgrim sounded harsh, pierced the air with coldness, and melted somewhere above the earth like the swollen voice of complaints that arose from the earth on that wonderful full moon.

I could not sleep that night. I shut my eyes as I lay on straw in the sexton's room, but it was in vain. Orgies of lights, colors, and sounds and the accents of sobs funneled through my brain in contours that were mobile like mists and covered some dark work that wove itself somewhere under the line of consciousness with their turbulence. When dawn bleached the windows and began to pour cloudy light into the room, I walked out in order to feel a little refreshed. I felt immensely agitated and tired. It seemed as if all my joints had fused together, and so I could move neither my legs nor my arms.

While I washed in some puddle, I heard the raised voices of some sisters in the room. They were arguing heatedly.

"You, sister, go to bed and wake up without saying a prayer, just like an animal!"

"Who are you to call me an animal?! Why don't you just lay off my comb and not touch my basket?"

"Right now, I am going to kneel and pray that God does not punish you, sister, for what you have just said."

"You won't fool yourself with prayers."

"Have mercy on unrepentant sinners, O Lord," she whispered as she knelt on the doorstep.

Meanwhile, the second sister, who wore a veil, got riled up and yelled:

"Look at her, that Pharisee! An old antiphon! What a hag!"

I left the women, paid twenty groszy for my lodging, and departed.

The cold stung my skin. Frost had whitened the bridges and fences, while fat drops of dew had turned the bent-over wheat gray, which was as silent as if it were in a dream.

We walked past nothing other than fruit gardens for quite some time. Bluish grayness was everywhere. Later, whitish mists slowly hovered over the ponds that flanked both sides of the road. Tattered pieces of the mists harshly swayed like stacks of wet, coarse canvas. I trotted so quickly that I was completely warm after ten minutes. The company had spread out so much that I saw people and carriages stretching out over three versts. They walked huddled and shivering from the cold, and besides it was the third day of the pilgrimage, which had taken its toll on their bodies.

It was four o'clock and I was getting so hungry I could barely stand it; I had no provisions, and I did not remember seeing a single inn since Grójec. I tried to feast on the views, but I stopped looking as soon as I saw the three veiled figures pass me. I tried to study them, but it was in vain. I only detected the lines of a beautiful profile and a serious gait in the tallest of them. A multitude of pilgrims walked, but without saying a word.

"Brother, where are we going now?" a short and red-haired brother asked.

"I don't know, but maybe one of these sisters does?" I asked shyly.

Three heads shook without uttering a word. The brother told me that he had been writing down the names of all the towns we had passed since Warsaw and took out a gray notebook filled with very careful handwriting.

"You have beautiful handwriting, brother."

The peasant grew red and said with a certain pride:

"Nobody ever taught me. Apart from reading and writing, I am skilled at carpentry; I can make a carriage and build a house. I also treat cattle. I have a subscription to the *Zorza* newspaper, which the courier brings, and I read. Our priest sometimes encouraged me to write them a letter about what goes on in our village. I wrote it and the priest sent it to the newspaper."

"Did they print it?" I asked with sincere interest.

"They printed everything, brother."

He raised his proudly radiating eyes and looked at me with sweetness. I encouraged him to write down all his experiences during the pilgrimage and upon returning home type them up and send them to *Zorza*'s editors.

"Would I know how to do so, brother?" he asked, beaming with sudden enchantment on his face.

I tried to explain to him how he could do that.

"You must be a writer for a newspaper, huh?" he asked loudly.

The three veiled profiles turned slightly, and so I felt their glance on me.

I denied that and did my best to try and correct him. We began to talk about something else, but I felt that my brother was nonetheless intimidated, because he kept calling me "sir." I left him and stayed at the end of the company. The sun had risen a little, and it sowed gold on the bright green barley and sucked the dew from the wheat. Delicate feathers slowly straightened up, while larks sang joyfully above the fields. Far away, ploughs dragged across the soil, which was golden-black from the sun, and their blades shone and flashed like silver thunder. A cluster of cattle was grazing in the meadow that a bluish creek cut across. Every time mooing came from there, the sound of reed pipes came from the willow trees whose young shoots flew up into the air. It was very peaceful there, as if sadness from the forests had scattered over the fields and closed the horizon. We only awoke the space with our crowd and our singing, which uninterruptedly resounded above our heads. Once again, a dust that made it impossible to breathe rose up, covering and obscuring everything. Thus, I constantly hit or stepped on the bare feet of some sister. Almost all the sisters walked barefoot; the rest wore stockings with canvas sewed to the soles or bast shoes. Most of the men wore either clogs or bast shoes. Only the Praga brothers paraded in gaiters. They walked freely, somehow not feeling tired. In the carriage next to me a plump, sturdy woman was seated and sang with the aid of a book. The pilgrims directly in front of her were singing something else; the woman did not care, though, but crowed in some strange soprano. A male voice that sounded very weak and gentle spoke to her from the carriage stall. The woman turned around and asked:

"Antoś,[1] are you all right?"

"I'm fine, Mom," someone whispered from the depths of the carriage. The pilgrims continued to sing.

I looked under the stall. A young fellow of about twenty was covered in blankets. A yellow face did not distinguish itself very well from his colorful pillowcase. He sang and moved the beads of a rosary with his dry fingers as he looked at the fields in front of him.

"Antoś, are you all right?"

"I'm good, Mom."

1 Antoś is the diminutive form of Antoni, the Polish form of Anthony.

They finished praying Lauds. With exceptionally delicate care, the mother embraced him through the blanket and tenderly gazed into his eyes.

"He's sick, dear brother," she said, having noticed me. "We're going to ask the Blessed Mother for mercy; maybe she will have mercy on the weak..."

"Mom, what's that blue stuff?" the sick boy asked, pointing at a tuft of young knapweeds growing by the roadside as his black eyes glistened with desire.

I picked as many as I could and brought them to him. He gave me a shy look and lovingly touched them with his mouth. This gesture surprised me; it seemed too soft for a male soul. He noticed this, because he looked at me and whispered softly, as if he were embarrassed:

"I like touching flowers so much that when I do touch them, I feel weak."

"Don't talk, Antoś. You see, brother, the doctors say he shouldn't talk."

"Has your son been ill for a long time?"

The mother responded by telling me the whole story of his illness.

"Two years ago, when he got back from Brazil, he lay down and started coughin' and coughin', and now he's drying up. If any animal or human would hurt my boy, I'd strangle 'em, even though my hands are weak. I have to watch him die and I can't do anything about it! Doctors and medicine cost a thousand zlotys. If the Blessed Virgin doesn't save him, then we will die together, because I will be left alone, and I never want to be alone."

"Mommy, you will dance at my wedding," the sick youth whispered as he caressed his mother's large hand with a kind of sad consolation.

"I wouldn't let him go to Brazil. I tried to barricade the doors and whimpered like a puppy, but he didn't listen; he wanted to go, and so he went. What good was it, brother? He has a beautiful profession, carpentry, land, and a house that he inherited from his father, and me alone, but he went across the ocean like a Jew or a criminal who can't look into the eyes of people here."

"Brother, how pretty they are," the ill pilgrim said as he pointed to pear trees sprinkled with flowers that were scattered across the fields.

"I cried; boy, did I cry. He was there for a year and then came back. I was feverishly happy, invited the neighbors, and slaughtered a piglet that didn't want to suckle the sow but was worth about three rubles, and I put on quite a ball for him! Do you remember, Antoś?"

"I remember, Mom."

Once again that pale, loving, and anemic smile blossomed on his mouth, but his mother suddenly changed the course of the conversation and briefly said:

"Antoś, they haven't invoked your patron saint yet."

She opened her book and read aloud, while the sick youth repeated every word with the unique attention and focus that are characteristic of tuberculosis patients.

I was about to leave when a long, well-bred arm stretched out in front of me and threw a blossoming pear branch and a blue bundle of pansies on the ill man's chest. It was one of the veiled women; she was so close that I detected a wonderful profile and the blue glimmer of pupils from behind her muslin veil.

She had obviously heard our conversation.

8

Łęczeszyce

THIS WAS A SHORT BREAK. A CHURCH THAT
had once been an abbey with an Italianate facade stood near
the road, almost in the wheat field. Modest on the inside,
this was a church for ploughmen who would come from
these humming fields, kneel in the wheat and on the road,
and pray facing a cross and the pale figures of the saints
that had been painted on the walls but were so pale and
spiritual in their expressions and tone that they seemed to
be mere phantasms floating above the fields at noon. These
were merely the notions of shapes and bodies.

The former monastery building was a ruin. Small open-
ings that had previously served as windows recalled ocular
orbits; they were empty and torn up, and they breathed
sadness and silence. Hens clucked and a gang of chicks
chirped and wallowed in the sand. Several large trees were
dying, breathing their last outside the church. When the
priest began to speak from behind the altar to us after Mass,
a drawn-out hiss shook the church.

"They're possessed!" the crowd cried, and a veritable
cyclone, a cloud of bodies thrashing around in all directions surrounded the unfortunate souls.

Someone walked them past me.

The priest went on, but I walked out. Two spasmatic
bodies were writhing in the sand by the road. They tossed
around like epileptics and moved around like rabid animals; they tore off the clothes they were wearing and
chewed the soil and pebbles. Next, they would pause for a
moment and fall on their backs, convulsing, foaming at the
mouth, and giving terrifying, long wails. They panted for
a while and their bloodshot eyes glimmered. One of them
jumped on the brother closest to her, ripped the rosary off

his neck, tore up his book, and began to jerk, stomp her feet, and howl.

"God, huh? All this holy rubbish and Mary? Ha, ha, ha!" she cackled in a rather frightening way. "You fool! The Devil is God! I am God! I am the Devil!" She started to wallow once more and whimper briefly, crawl on her belly, and kick sand.

Everyone was overcome with a kind of horror.

This crowd stood in helpless silence, seemingly crushed by an immeasurable weight. Their faces were filled with sadness, fear, and desolation. They bent their necks as if they unwittingly knew that the bright roof of the heavens could fall on them at any moment.

The possessed ceased moving.

Their bloodshot eyes began to look at the faces in the crowd; they breathed heavily, and they seemed to wake, because some flashes of awakening awareness flickered in their eyes. For a moment, they stood in the sun, covered in blood and dust with their faces ragged, tattered rags thrown over them, and a stare that expressed immense pain, despair, and a call for help; the crowd slowly moved away from the force of that terrifying sight and fearfully huddled together.

A tall peasant with a very genteel and powerful stare stepped out of the circle, walked up to the possessed, grabbed them by the shoulders with his strong arm, and made them kneel on the ground.

"Pray, brothers and sisters, for these possessed souls. Pray for them!"

The crowd knelt.

Prayers, sighs, moans, and sobs rustled; they began to get up and surrounded these two souls like a wheel of harmony and empathy, a mystical sphere of hymns and pleas. The peasant, however, made sure they were kneeling and solemnly said:

"Repeat after me, sisters!"

They tried to jump up, but he only increased his grip on them.

"You are children of Mary. We believe in God and ask for His mercy. We reject the Devil and impure thoughts."

"We are children of Mary...," they repeated softly and slowly, accentuating regret. This moved the hearts of the people, whose sobs were growing louder.

"And You, Lord, who are in heaven and on earth and in every star and in every pebble and in the smallest blade of grass and everywhere, have mercy on us for our sins!"

They repeated after him, but they grew softer and foggier, because tears began to fall from their faces and their bodies began to tremble. They stretched their arms towards the sun and amid momentary flashes of consciousness began to beg for mercy and succor from the depths of their hearts and blood. It was as if all these hearts had united in their pleas, because streaks of tears flowed down all their eyes, a single moan resounded, and increasingly zealous prayers said with more and more emphasis burst out in the sunny silence.

I could hear nothing but that choir of sobbing voices begging for mercy.

One of the possessed began to scream and jump up; she pushed the peasant away with such force that he fell on the fence. They began to wail and blaspheme once more. The convulsions returned, but they did not last as long. They had quickly exhausted their strength and fell unconsciously. A couple of brothers walking at the end of the pilgrimage who had been hired by the company picked them up and took the possessed to carriages.

Someone told me that these women were from the Lublin region, but I could learn little more than that "the Devil came inside them" when they saw Masses or priests. The pilgrims began to tell me about dozens of similar cases. I stopped listening, because the sobs of those people and their simple and sincere pleas began to choke me.

I let people and carriages filled with the blind, crippled, and paralyzed, those afflicted by infirmities for which humans have no cure, pass me. That caravan of wounded

41

bodies and souls, that terrible theater of life moved like a dream filled with tormenting apparitions.

I saw and felt through those thick covers, those emaciated masks that were their faces; I was almost completely aware of the state of their souls and their suffering. I could tell that they weren't taking a mere walk; I knew why they were walking. My skeptical, ironic "I," which had been bred in a cramped cell of urban life, receded with fear and admiration; it stood flabbergasted and uncertain among so many sufferings, so many concerns, so much pain... I saw and felt that there was scarcely a heart, soul, or head that did not carry the yoke of misery in that crowd, that did not walk trusting God and believing that they would receive everything if they placed their tears before the Blessed Virgin and told her of their pain, opening their aching hearts and asking for succor and mercy. What would all these souls, pains, complaints, sufferings, and miseries do if, all of a sudden, they were overcome by the darkness of doubt and knew not where to go, what to believe, and whom to entrust themselves to with this limitless trust?

My soul grew dark and frightened as I pondered this, and I felt that we were like the reeds in the ponds that dried up during the summer and whose yellow bunches fluttered in the nights, sun, and spring: "Everything's dead! It's dead!" Only they had died, because everything around was brimming with life, blossoming, and singing; it suffered, but it was alive. I felt their tears!

I ran to catch up to the brothers and walked with them in the unmerciful heat. The road passed by a pine forest; it smelled of resin dried by the heat, which poured into our breasts. The young birch leaves produced such fragrance that the whole company walked more slowly and ponderously. The heat, the silence of the forest, the songs whose echoes spread across the forest, the sleepless night, and the diverse sensations made me sleepy and prone to hallucinatory daydreaming. Clouds of dust covered everything and rose up above the forest, so at times it seemed as if these voices were coming from the ground; that these songs, which swam across forest crossroads, moved tree crowns and young ferns, and soaked in the soil that exhaled chilly darkness, were supernatural in origin.

I barely made it to where we would be spending the night.

9

Mogielnica

MOGIELNICA IS AN AVERAGE TOWN, NO different from thousands like it.

Through foggy sleepiness, I recall many houses whose gables faced the streets and whose arcades rested on carved blocks that acted as columns. The church was in the cemetery outside city limits; everyone else went there, but because I was too tired, I lay down in the shadow of a linden next to a pile of bricks that were intended for the construction of a new church and fell sound asleep.

I slept for around three hours, finally awakened by the singing of departing brothers. I quickly ate something in some inn and got back on the road again.

We had to walk thirteen versts to Nowe Miasto on the Pilica River.

The area was increasingly undulant, and the soil was poor. The shabby, low, and dirty houses in the poor villages were striking in their ugliness and abandonment; the vegetation was also much poorer. Instead of cottonwood trees, there were irregularly and shabbily planted willow trees by the road. The people there were somehow cloudy, emaciated, and drably dressed; they did not make a very pleasant impression. Poverty was evident on their faces. Even the foliage was somehow flaxen, because sand shone amid the sparsely planted rye and oats.

There was not a blade of wheat in the fields.

A couple versts past Mogielnica, we walked past a pasture filled with cattle and gaggles of geese, because there was a small brook of rust-filled water with swamps exposing tufts of rush and yellow ducklings. A gang of children tending cattle ran towards us and knelt with folded hands. Sisters affectionately gave slices of bread and lumps of sugar to the children, but they continued to kneel. I passed the last child who got the least from the pilgrims; she grabbed my sleeve and begged in a slender voice:

"Give me something, O pious brother!"

I gave her a couple groszy and thought that the children had been taught to beg, because they were five years old at the most; their blue eyes and pretty, clean faces could not mask their cunning expressions.

It was getting hotter, but the road was good, and I had slept well, so I somehow managed to continue walking. I heard fewer conversations and complaints; the pilgrims were silent or sang, as the heat was not conducive to chitchat.

I saw the three veiled women, who walked with difficulty near the end of the procession.

All of them had an ashen hue because their faces had not become tan from the sun; instead, they were growing blue and taking on the color of the road.

A couple umbrellas rocked above their heads; I offered mine to the three veiled women, but they once again responded by gently and silently shaking their heads.

They're not Varsovians! I thought to myself.

They deliberately walked without umbrellas. I walked away, but I was fascinated by their mysteriousness. The profile of the tallest one, which I had noticed through the fog of the veil, depressed me. I realized she resembled Isis in her layered veil.

The elevation of the winding road varied. Outside Nowe-Miasto, it was so steep that the drivers were asked to stop the carriages and ride later in order to prevent a possible accident. If they could, those riding in the wagons had to get off as well.

We got up to the second peak of the plateau, from which we could see Nowe-Miasto and the broadly glistening ribbon of the Pilica River on the left. Past the river, there were forests as far as the eye could see. I felt cooler just from the thought that we soon would walk through forests, because we were baking in the sun. Those who could do so took off some of their clothes and placed them on the wagons to make walking easier. Even some of the Praga brothers discreetly took their leggings off in a ditch.

10

Nowe-Miasto

THE CAPUCHIN CHURCH AND ABBEY WERE in the exact same style and internal arrangement as that on Miodowa Street in Warsaw.

We were greeted by tons of tables and simmering samovars spread out on the market square in front of the church. Several smaller companies were also resting.

After visiting the church, which was very clean and was decorated with plenty of flowers at the altar, I went to get some tea. The veiled women sat down at the neighboring table; two of them slightly uncovered their veils, but not on the side that I could see. I offered them my services, because I could tell from their drawn-out accents that they were not from Warsaw. They turned down my offer, but they rewarded my politeness with a lemon slice for my tea. Since I had accepted the lemon slice with gratitude, I tried to strike up a conversation, but it did not flow.

The three-day walk had been so exhausting that I did not know what to talk about.

I went to visit the abbey. In the corridor, I picked up a wooden, cross-shaped handle and rang the bell. A crippled boy opened the door. I asked to see Father Prokop. He led me up to the first floor.

The omnipresent cleanliness was astounding.

A bit hesitant, I stood in front of low doors with the inscription: "J.S.V. Procopus."[1] I asked if I could enter and, having received an affirmative response, walked in.

The cell was square with calcium-bleached walls and a simple, pine floor.

---

1 Prokop in Latin.

Above all, I saw poverty and a lack of the most important accessories. A simple couch covered by a thick blanket made of fur served as a bed and was under a wall adorned with a black cross. I saw nothing more, because my vision was arrested by an old man sitting in a low, wooden chair between two windows. His large, grayish pupils seemed to penetrate me with an immeasurably deep stare, while an elongated, ascetic head, bleached somewhat by gray hair, wrinkled forehead, and harsh face that seemed to have congealed in long and sharp wrinkles intimidated me somewhat. The first cenobitic monks must have had that same expression of calm asceticism and wisdom.

I introduced myself in a few words. There were several moments of silence, after which I felt the old man's serious and investigative glance on me; apart from that, I noticed two large books bound in sheepskin lying on a reed table and several pages of a manuscript covered in very harsh and exuberant handwriting. After that, I heard a subdued but melodic voice invite me to sit down.

I pulled up a chair and sat directly across from him.

The conversation I refer to below is not a literal transcription; it is exact neither in form nor in content.

"What's new in the world? What's new in literature? We here feed only off echoes," he asked; I saw that he had a very benevolent and pleasant smile.

I replied to him. We spoke about different movements in literature and science and the reaction that was conducive to Catholicism and faith and which could be felt everywhere.

"It had to come to that eventually. That's all the better for those who will see it soon. What are these legends about the Virgin Mary that Mr. Gawalewicz[2] has written about?"

---

2 Marian Gawalewicz (1852–1910) was a Polish writer whose works included the compilation *Królowa niebios. Legendy ludowe o Matce Boskiej* ("Queen of the Heavens: Folk Legends about the Virgin Mary"), which was first published in 1894.

I summarized some of them to him; he listened attentively and said:

"Yes. That is the purest poetry of feeling that I know. The
souls of our people best express themselves about this. Mary
is a brook that quenches all those who are weary."

He looked ahead of himself profoundly, after which he
returned to the aim of my pilgrimage, which I had men-
tioned to him at the beginning.

"This was a good idea, but you should not become dis-
couraged or judge this mass based on some of its shenani-
gans, which are inevitable during such a long journey with
so many people. Forgive their coarseness, their ugly words,
their crass behavior, and the wicked individuals, whom you
can find everywhere. You have to look deeper, into their
hearts. What are your impressions so far?"

"They are very deep. Above all, I have come to believe
in their profound faith."

"Their faith is deep, and their hearts have yet to be cor-
rupted. They are the wisest of the wise, because they believe.
They do not ask, doubt, or inquire — they believe. That is
the key to their strength and their joy."

"Today, I envied their ability to believe and the power
that flows from their faith."

"Not only should we envy them, but you should weep
about such a loss," he said firmly. I said nothing, because I
began to be overwhelmed with a kind of bitterness.

"In reality, it's you who don't believe in God or in people;
in spirit nor in matter. They've blinded themselves and say
that nothing exists, because they see nothing. O, pitiful folly!
The brash madness of moles!"

"Father," I said, "do you think that this happens without
leaving a trace, that it is a delight to not know and not
even have any place where one's thoughts can find solace?"

"I know, and so I pity vain sufferings all the more."

He slightly lowered his head and nervously stroked his
beard, after which he inhaled some snuff that he had taken

out of a black case with a beautiful enamel image of the Assumption of the Virgin Mary on the cover. He spoke for a long time and concluded by saying:

"The source of unhappiness is within us, in our reason, but the source of peace and joy is there!"

He pointed at the Christ stretched over his bed with his wiry arm.

"Go and drink from the source of truth and good, and you will regain yourselves and find what you cannot find anywhere else. Sacred Scripture says: 'Come to me, all you who labor and are burdened, and I will give you rest.' Why, then, is there so much struggle and conflict? Why do we lose our souls and those of others when happiness is near us, when it is a visible aim, while life is so fleeting?"

We were silent for a long time. I masticated these words that breathed with the gravity of a deep faith, while Father Prokop once again looked at the image of Christ on the wall, slightly moved his lips as if he were praying, and finally asked:

"Where will you print your impressions of the pilgrimage?"

"In *Tygodnik Ilustrowany*."

"May God bless you and help you in your good work. I wish this to all the pilgrims, and I wish you to be strong and persistent. Drink from the source; that is where you will find consolation and happiness!"

I got ready to leave.

"I won't keep you because it's time for my prayers; I don't go to the choir because my legs are good for nothing."

I kissed his hand goodbye because he had won me over with his bright, venerable age. Father Prokop, meanwhile, kissed me on the head, made the sign of the cross over me, and imperceptibly whispered something.

I walked out and immediately stood in the corridor in order to sum up my impressions, but that serene face lingered in my brain. I constantly heard that deep voice telling me:

"Drink from the source; that is where you will find consolation and happiness!"

I slowly walked through the corridors. The faded faces of friars gazed at me from the paintings that adorned the walls. I saw gray beards, dimmed eyes, harsh facial features, ascetic bodies, and souls full of self-denial and submission; in the bronze frames, I saw naively painted scenes that were nonetheless full of spirited feeling, where simple and tired souls initially leaned out; the tragedy of struggle against oneself and sacrificing one's life; tumultuous scenes of murders, where the murdered had smiles of inexpressible joy; where there were ascetic philosophers, laudably abnegated souls, hearts aflame with just one feeling, ecstatic exaltation, divine smiles of harshness and benevolence, and nameless expressions of suffering. Popes, cardinals, bishops, simple monks, benefactors of the abbey in steel armor; beings that were broken in the silence of the cell and looked for oblivion.

This was a hecatomb of sacrifices and offerings. A whole procession of souls and the shadows of bodies that had long become dispersed across the universe — all this seemed to move, step out from these canvasses, move in the lights of the corridors, softly sing hymns, move past me, and whisper while pointing at the cross stretched above the window:

"That is where you will find consolation and happiness!"

As I walked out, I heard the friars in the abbey choir singing the soft tones of a hymn. I went to the garden and took in, not only the beauty of springtime nature, but also the calm that was present there as well as that silence of some sweet life of isolation and dedication to a single ideal, the silence of hearts that believed and found the kingdom of oblivion in isolation from the world.

For a long time, I sat under the apple trees whose pink flowers fell at my feet. I listened to the delicate, dying murmurs of singing and found within me a very old and very strong desire: to be alone and to rest. At that moment, I thought that this abbey would bring solace and joy to many sick and weary souls; it would be a quiet wharf for those who had been crushed by the wheel of fate.

I saw the two possessed women in the sacristy; they had gone to confession. They were kneeling, lucid and steeped in prayer. I only saw their blue, swollen faces and expressions of great sadness in their teary eyes.

After that, I never saw them again.

Nowe-Miasto is above all an unkempt and tattered town. Its clinic failed to impress me. A new park was a skimpy collection of lousy trees that looked as if they were in need of hydrotherapy and had been planted on the incline of a hill. The buildings were dumpy and had not a trace of beauty in their contours. A long veranda intended for concerts or other performances but that, in practice, was usually used for the purpose of taking walks on rainy days, was strikingly ugly and in a terrible state of disrepair. There were muddy meadows that were completely devoid of any fragrance below the house of the clinic director. I felt that I could not live there for even a week, as the boring and ugly surroundings would overwhelm me. Perhaps I disliked this work of human hands so intensely because my eyes and brain had been dazzled by the royal grandeur of the fields and forests.

I ran into some brothers who were getting ready to leave. I looked for the veiled women and we walked together on a very steep, snaking road that had been cut in the soil all the way to the Pilica River.

A park to our right rose above an incline and stretched over the Pilica. It was already seven in the evening; the air had ceased to be hot and a cool breeze came from that mass of trees and the water. We walked across a bridge over the Pilica, a broad river with plenty of sandbanks and rafts in the current.

There was a very pretty view of the park, the parish church atop a hill, and the clinic; on the other bank, which was flat and overgrown with trees, the monotony of the view was tedious.

After we had passed the river, we moved to a country road off to the right that stretched across slender pastures that at some points were sprinkled with heaps of sand. Later, we walked across only a sandy road that cut across pine groves and what remained of high forests. Some of the heavier carriages went on the road; we would only see them two days later in Wielko-Wola.

Everyone looked terribly exhausted; the six miles we had done that day were taking a toll on me as well.

The veiled women spoke in monosyllables and walked on a harder path in the forest, but I walked along the road because I could not feel the toughness of the roots as much. In order to kill time, I tried to guess the faces from their profiles, which I could barely see through the veils; I wanted to summarize them for myself and define each one.

The first, who was also the tallest, walked slowly and slightly hunched-over. Exhaustion was evident from the lines of her figure, while her expression was full of silent sadness. I studied the glance of her huge eyes, which were submerged in a dreamy state and which I had already seen before; her smile, which was exceedingly kind, but nonetheless enigmatically sad; and the gravity of the pride of her natural soul that did not feel happy there.

Yes, this was the personification of Melancholy.

The second was Contradiction; I saw this in every movement, word, and line of her posture. Contradiction was very pleasant and active, but she constantly stood in one spot because of constant internal changes and strikethroughs.

The third, meanwhile, was the resolute Pensiveness. She walked nearly automatically, and the line of her body was as perfectly wavelike in calm movement as a Greek frieze depicting the *kanephoros*.[3] She held her head in front of

---

3 A decorative motif originating in ancient Greece that depicted a woman carrying a basket of flowers or fruit on her head or shoulders.

her; I could swear that her wide-open eyes saw none of her surroundings because she was so lost in thought.

We were silent and surrounded by growing silence all around us.

Murmurs of the night, slowly dispersing shadows and grayness, quaked in the air along with the echoes of the singing of the company, which was walking far ahead of us. A cuckoo began to call from a thicket, which was odd given how late it was, while the whistling of blackbirds resounded from somewhere above the Pilica River.

These three bright figures began to eclipse the dusk and scatter its contours; they took on specter-like shapes and became foggy; it was as if they were merging with the depths of the forest, which hallucinated only the fogs of outlines and was filled with lines melting into the night.

We said nothing, because in the quiet of the night it was so good to dream incomplete dreams that swam across the paths of the afterglow of the sunset that still painted gold over the forests; to coil one's thoughts around the trees; to lie down on the branches that silently rustled the song of the night; to rock in transparent fogs and to let one's soul swell with the melancholy of that silence and the enlightening dream of a wizard rich in visions.

Photo 1: Pilgrims in folk costume on the way from Łowicz to Często-chowa. May 22, 2010. (Credit: Przykuta / CC BY-SA)

Photo 2: The 307th Walking Pilgrimage from Warsaw to Częstochowa. August 14, 2018. Credit: EpiskopatNews. Photo: Jasna Góra/Krzysztof Świertok. (CC BY-NC-SA 2.0)

Photo 3: Cardinal Kazimierz Nycz, Archbishop of Warsaw, with Pauline fathers and pilgrims. August 14, 2018. Credit: EpiskopatNews. Photo: Jasna Góra/Krzysztof Świertok. (CC BY-NC-SA 2.0)

Photo 4: The 27th Walking Pilgrimage from Zaolzie in Silesia. July 20, 2017. Credit: EpiskopatNews. Photo: Marek Kępiński. (CC BY-NC-SA 2.0)

Photo 5: Walking Pilgrimage from Wadowice, hometown of Pope St. John Paul II. July 19, 2017. Credit: EpiskopatNews. Photo: Krzysztof Świertok. (CC BY-NC-SA 2.0)

Photo 6: Pilgrims from Wadowice, hometown of Pope St. John Paul II, prostrating in front of Jasna Góra. July 19, 2017. Credit: EpiskopatNews. Photo: Krzysztof Świertok. (CC BY-NC-SA 2.0)

Photo 7: The 38th Pilgrimage of Defenders of Life. April 7, 2018. Credit: EpiskopatNews. Photo: Krzysztof Świertok. (CC BY-NC-SA 2.0)

Photo 8: 1987, during the Solidarity period. Banner reads: "Freedom, Love, Peace"

11

Różanna

OUR BROTHERS HAD ALREADY GONE TO sleep by the time we arrived.

The veiled women already had accommodations that had been prepared by the company's mother, while I went to find a place to spend the night.

This was a small village, and there wasn't enough lodging in all its barns and shacks for all the pilgrims, so many of them went to sleep in gardens and backyards.

After an exhausting search, I finally found a corner in a room full of sisters. They were in good spirits, because laughter and bawdy jokes reverberated across the room. Only occasionally could I hear pious songs from the barn, but other than that it was mostly babble and the noisiness of a primeval encampment.

I sat at the doorstep and brooded. I was a bit frustrated because I was very hungry, but there was nowhere I could buy milk or bread; in fact, there wasn't even any water left in the well! Just then, though, a sister offered me a slice of bread and said:

"Take it, brother, and eat it!" Another sister brought cheese, another still brought me butter; soon enough, I had honey, a scrap of cured meat, and a big pancake topped with cinnamon.

Before I had come to my senses after this surprise, I was sitting in the middle of the room in the company of about forty sisters. I began to thank them and wanted to leave, because this had touched me so much. They would not let me leave, however.

"Eat, brother; don't be shy. We are all one and the same. We see that although you are gentry you walk piously and give a good example; what more can I do than cut bread and give you some?"

I had a good meal and ate the cinnamon pancake with honey. I found milk in some canteen.

Later, I followed the host and quietly told him that I would pay for everyone's lodging. One of the pilgrims overheard this and said:

"Brother, you wanted to hurt good souls by repaying a good heart with some groszy; this is neither kind nor noble!"

I tried to explain myself as best as I could, but they did not want to listen; each of them immediately began to pay their four groszy.

"Brother, you can repay us by reading us something from this book," one of them said and gave me an old copy of the New Testament bound in leather and with a rosary tied around it.

I began to read from the Acts of the Apostles.

I read various things that came from different places. I read other people's works and my own writings, private and public; never before had I had such stage fright and such an attentive audience at the same time. There was a throng of people outside the house and the room was crowded, as reading aloud fortified the spirits of the people, who listened attentively. Every so often, I had to answer questions and explain passages or make them more accessible.

I read for about an hour.

They made me an honorary bed on a chest, which was very comfortable; we went to bed and that was how the third night of the pilgrimage passed.

When we were idling about in the morning, one sister said:

"You, brother, should be a priest. You're educated, you read beautifully, and you explained the Word of God in a way that entered every heart with sweetness. You would be consolation to both God and people."

I replied nothing as I washed in a bucket. I began to think of Warsaw, my nighttime adventures in the city with friends, our conversations, and the breaking up of rotten forms and institutions. I wanted to shout there to them: "Listen! Listen!"

We left the village with the cross at the fore of the procession and waited.

I asked what was happening. They told me that the previous day the elder brother saw licentiousness in several places, so he wanted to reprimand the pilgrims; after a moment, he stood alone in front of the cross.

The crowd huddled together and was silent. Dawn was breaking as a milky light emerged from this foggy, blue grayness, slowly seeping into the sky and bleaching the space.

Carriages were getting in front of the crowd; I noticed the three veiled women on one of them.

The first larks began to call in the air, while a stork standing in a nest atop a poplar tree twisted its neck and clacked for a long time. The cattle roared in the cowshed, begging for silage; the village was waking up.

The elder brother waited until everyone had arrived and began to speak. I will quote only several passages that I remember.

"Where are you going, brothers and sisters? Are you going to a bazaar? If so, why are you accompanied by a cross? Are you going to inns for parties or to a wedding? Then why do you sing such pious songs and use God's name? You are not going to a country fair, no! At night, there was plenty of laughter and frolicking that offended God! You are not headed for debauchery, but to the Blessed Mother. Do you not fear God's punishment, sisters and brothers? How can you not expect disease and death among cattle and people, that your villages will not burn down, hailstorms not descend, and devils will not kill you, but instead plentiful harvests, when through your behavior you show that that is exactly what you want?! Because of your vices and lack of restraint, God will lose His patience and send upon you famine, disease, and fire to burn out the evil. Then, beloved

brothers and sisters, you will weep, lament, and cry for succor. You are undisguised sinners with no restraint, yet you
want to go to the Most Blessed Virgin in this way! People,
come to your senses!"

He spoke in a resounding, pompous voice, while increasingly thick sobs slowly rose up. More and more people began
to kneel, beat their breasts, and beg the Lord for forgiveness.

The red ball that was the sun rolled across the sky,
obliquely throwing light on these dark faces, weary and
aflame with irritation. Meanwhile, the brother went on
speaking, finally concluding with:

"You will no longer be like animals that dig through anything or thickets of fragrant herbs or thistles. Come to your
senses, brothers and sisters, because you are walking to our
beloved Mother and you will arrive dirty, resembling cattle
rather than people. What will the Blessed Virgin say? That
you are not her children, only degenerate and loathsome
stepchildren! Amen."

He finished, took the cross, and intoned a hymn. We
walked in an immensely long line, because the road was
very narrow, and it snaked up a hill.

The whole group dispersed over the space of several
versts and flickered against the background of the wheat
fields like a colorful ribbon woven with bright colors.

The soil was barren and deforested; the trunks of
half-decayed trees were dark amid the fields of rye, while
tufts of juniper grew in the balk.

We walked quickly, because the morning chill was
refreshing, and we had recovered our strength after a good
night's sleep.

A chapel was atop a pointed hill in front of us. Behind
it was a huge forest, yellowed from afar by the trunks of
pine trees. It was half-covered by fogs rising from the sap
and swamps. Soon, I saw how the head of the procession
with the cross at the front climbed up the hill, paused for
a moment, and flowed sideways into the forest. This high

and low tide, this rope made of colorful knots strung in the gray forest path and sinking in the trees was exceptionally beautiful.

I waited for an hour or so for my turn.

That hill was so steep that legs alone were not enough to get up it; I had to aid myself with my arms, too.

This was an immemorial wooden chapel with a figure of St. Mary Magdalene cut into the wood with a frugal polychrome, decorated with curtains and clad in a coral necklace.

The women each took several pebbles from the peak and hid them with great reverence.

I asked what the chapel commemorated.

"St. Mary Magdalene built this hill with her own hands; she held every pebble, and they are good for toothaches."

"That's how it was, brother," a fellow pilgrim said after we had descended the hill. "Old people would say this. I heard about it thirty years ago. They said that this happened when St. Peter and Jesus walked the earth and told people how they should act in the world."

"Is that so, brother?" I asked, feigning surprise.

"Why wouldn't it be true? It's written down in books, and reliable people tell this story. I won't tell you exactly when this happened, but then it was like it is now: people were good, evil, or somewhere in between. I'll tell you how they told it to me. St. Peter bought a carriage and a horse, because the Lord Jesus' holy feet got injured and He couldn't walk. They sat down and ate. Being the host, Jesus sat in the back, while St. Peter sat in the front. They traveled the same road we're on now.

"The pebbles were piled up high, the horse was hot, and the wooden carriage kept creaking. Jesus couldn't say a prayer, because there was a constant creaking.

"So, He said: 'Check what's squeaking, Peter.'

"St. Peter wanted to sleep because of the heat, so he flogged the horse and replied: 'It's the pebbles under the wheels.'

"He remembered that he had to grease the carriage. Jesus grew annoyed. 'Stand and get up,' He said. St. Peter stopped the horse and got off. 'Take a hatchet and let's go.'

"They went into the forest. Jesus found a conifer tree and said: 'Cut it!' St. Peter cut down the tree. They melted tar, used it to grease the axles, and left. They kept riding until they found a skinny woman who lamented and begged them to take her. Jesus pretended He couldn't hear.

"And St. Peter said: 'The road is harsh, my lady; our horse is weak, and our carriage is shaking. You'll ruin your ankles. Follow the railroad tracks and you will make it to wherever you want. May you be healthy.'

"Jesus couldn't take it anymore, and so He said: 'Take her, Peter.'

"Peter replied: 'This is too much, my Lord, so someone will have to walk.'

"'Then you get off and walk!'

"St. Peter became morose and so he mumbled: 'Sit, woman, in the back of the carriage.' But she had already fallen asleep.

"'Where are you from?' Jesus asked. She cried and lamented and said her name was Magdalene and she walked the world in search of death because all the people had cast her off like a stray dog. Jesus immediately saw she was a great sinner.

"'You have sinned a lot!'

"She looked into those holy eyes at once and her heart shrunk out of fear, but she said: 'I am a sinner, Lord.'

"'Sin no longer, repent, and your sins will be forgiven!' The Lord Jesus told her to take handfuls of pebbles until she'd build a hill in the middle of the woods. St. Magdalene left to build a hill—the one we were just on—while the Lord Jesus and St. Peter left. They stopped to spend the night at a village that was on their way.

"The Lord Jesus gave St. Peter money and said: 'Peter, take ten coins and ask for some hay for the horse, because it's completely hungry, but don't let anyone hurt it, because that'd be a sin.' He went by himself to the chapel past the village to pray. St. Peter was left alone and felt as hungry as the horse, but he was poor. There was waist-high clover by the road and there was no one in the field. He let the horse off into the field and went inside the house to eat something. He ate, paid, and left. St. Peter tied a knot around the horse, which he let run off to the pasture, and wrapped a thick rope around his hand so that the horse wouldn't run away. Then he went to bed, having figured that by the time the Lord Jesus would come he would be rested, and the horse would have eaten.

"At night, the peasant came to take the horse away from him. St. Peter begged him, but the peasant was tough, and he wanted a gold coin for the trouble. St. Peter didn't have it, so they took him and locked him up in a chamber. Jesus came the following day for Lauds and called:

"'Peter! Peter!' But there was nothing. He could only hear whimpering behind the wall, so he called once more:

"'Peter! Peter!'

"St. Peter replied: 'When I came, Lord, this peasant locked me up in a chamber and didn't want to free me or the horse for a gold coin!'

"The Lord Jesus paid the coin and got angry, because the difference between leaving a horse to graze on someone else's pasture and harming one's neighbor is like that between stealing and killing. The peasant saw a brightness over the Lord Jesus' head and recognized that He was God, so he quickly came with his woman and children, gave Him back the gold coin, and asked:

"'Stay with us, Lord Jesus! The foal will be let out of the chamber, I will clean and bleach the chamber so it is all right, and the horse will have clover every day and the stable boy will have food to eat.'

"The Lord Jesus recognized that this peasant was a good person, so he quietly blessed him and said: 'Indeed, everyone will receive payment for what they have done. Take this gold coin, boy, because you need it for clover. There is not a king or lord who should pay for what he takes.' And He left."

"Maybe you know something more about the Lord Jesus, brother?" I asked, delighted by the naiveté of the tale.

"No, I don't know anything more."

I left him and went to the forest to be alone, because the trees were trying to tell me something and they summoned me into the depths of the forest. The psalmody of the people echoed; it was an increasingly soft wave that died out in a silvery whisper whose sound I followed. The forest was heated by glimmers of sunlight and began to pray in the silence of the golden dusk.

The biggest pines I have ever seen in my life stood like a forest of amber columns under a green roof with blue cutting through it.

Bee-eaters flew from branch to branch like red flashes; they flapped their wings and their prolonged cry resounded in the silence like the detached fragment of a nocturne.

Moss of an exceedingly soft emerald hue spread at the bottom of the forest like waters with calm depths. Whispers, clatters, fragrances, and murmurs walked across the space. Sometimes, the final echoes of songs stroked the mighty chords of the forest, reverberating in a beautiful, sweet melody that wrapped around the soul and dispersed it across the forest.

A mild, warm wind pushed through the trees, which silently quivered and rocked. The strange and unsettling blackness under the crowns of the extensive spruces rippled like a harsh rhythm in this magical forest symphony.

I shook because a harsh scale of singing caught up to me like a brutal, cold streak of February light and disrupted this sacred silence with a screeching hubbub and din, while words I had once read swarmed in my brain:

I hear noise, and I hear moans,
I hear trembling voices nigh;
Ominous fear makes my heart groan,
And dew fills my eye.

The company stopped to rest right outside the forest,
from which we went to Studzianna together.
We got there by eight in the morning.
A priest greeted us with music, banners, and feretories.
After giving a speech, he invited us into the church.

12

Studzianna

THE CHURCH IN THIS VILLAGE USED TO BE an abbey belonging to the Oratorian Fathers and had been built in a decadent Renaissance style. It had a Baroque altar. This was a large, luminous church with three naves and faded frescoes on the ceiling. Rows of portraits of princes of the Church and knights hung in the dark sacristy.

Two portraits in particular caught my eye: one depicted a cardinal and the other a knight in full armor and a lynx cape.

The church complex was huge and well-tended; behind them were gardens cut off from the rest of the world by a high wall.

I studied the church once more and concluded that it had been built in the seventeenth century but, based on the bombastic kitschy decorations, it must have been adapted to its current state in the eighteenth. What annoyed me about almost every country church, particularly in these parts, were the statues; they were simply awful. The carpentry was truly barbaric, gilded and polychromed by the eunuchs of art.

I went back to the sacristy.

There was a crowd by the altar; they were buying pictures and books describing the church and the miraculous Lady of Studzianna. By the time I had reached the portraits, I heard:

"Brothers and sisters, you are a drove of cattle. As God is my witness, you lack humanity; you push and shove past one another like a herd."

I did not see who among the crowd was saying this.

I liked this portrait less because I saw that the painter had hidden his powerlessness behind trickery, dull and powdery coloration, and the pompous pose of the cardinal who stood as if he demanded that all the simpletons admire him. This tacky and flat method of painting reminded me of marionettes clad in tailcoats and crowns, Poniatowski-era[1] dandies painted by Bacciarelli's[2] pupils. The painter did not understand the body, unlike during the Renaissance, and there was not a subtle expression or thought as in da Vinci's art; instead, he painted only according to unchanging patterns. Bishops, kings, knights, nobles.... He presented them all in their ceremonial pomp and lavishness.

Having ceased looking at the one in armor, I left the church and studied the beggars.

This was a mine of ugliness and monstrosity. This colorful gang stood on both sides of the path. I counted thirty-two blind, crippled, mute, and hobbled mendicants. It was clear that they were old professionals from how they stretched out their arms and flaunted their disability.

They begged in stupendous voices, bent over, and moaned for at least one grosz from the pious brothers and sisters; each one proclaimed he was the most unfortunate of them all.

It was a mine of characters, movements, snickers, moans, and apostolic glances; the expressions of villainous faces and a rubbish heap of disgusting souls, because I could tell from a mile away that this was a pose, a masquerade of beggary, disgusting cynicism, and the duplicity of professionals. Only one among this filthy mob looked different. He was truly

1   Stanisław August (Stanislaus Augustus) Poniatowski was the last king of the Polish-Lithuanian Commonwealth, reigning from 1764 to 1795. He was a major champion of the Enlightenment, being the patron of art and political reforms inspired by Enlightenment thought, including the adoption of Europe's first written constitution (the Constitution of May 3, 1791).

2   Marcello Bacciarelli (1731–1818) was an Italian late Baroque and early neo-Classicist painter who was invited to Warsaw by King Poniatowski to be the director of the Academy of Arts and director of the Royal Buildings and Estates. He also painted several paintings for the Polish monarchy which can be seen today in the Royal Castle in Warsaw.

blind and sang without end, while an old woman sitting next to him echoed him in a falsetto. I sat behind this pair to hear what they were singing.

Fewer people were coming out of the church, while my beggar was singing:

> *Is the end of the world comin'?*
> *A son takes over his father's estate,*
> *Mother and daughter hate*
> *One another; It's strange you're*
> *   not in hell by this date,*
> *Devil woman!*

Later, he sang variants of the same song.

"Stop singing idly, you fool," the woman whispered to him, albeit loud enough for me to hear everything. "Nobody's coming anymore."

He grew silent and started to count his money.

"One ruble. A wage like that is good for a dog. Those filthy, wretched scoundrels are going on a pilgrimage without money, like complete failures."

He spat derisively, took out his snuff box, and said:

"Take some, woman, because you've worked hard enough."

I walked away so I would not disturb this hard worker's well-deserved rest.

There were plenty of people in the square in front of the church. A company from Zwoleń outside Radom was coming; it was about a thousand souls who walked with a priest and banners at the fore. The people were tall and had intelligent faces. The women had handkerchiefs wrapped around their heads like turbans, fleece, and white-striped blue cloaks hanging from their shoulders.

Their dress, accent, and somehow greater liveliness distinguished them from us.

Although the rest had gone to the church, I was very hungry, so I went to the square to get some food. The cabbage soup was disgusting, and the tea was even worse, but that was all there was.

I slept on the turf in the priests' garden in the shadow of the apple tree, which was completely covered in flowers and bees making honey. I went to the pond, which was dirty and polluted with clay, to bathe at least a little bit. Quite a few people were bathing by the bank.

A sister scooped out some butter on a rag, studied her pot in the sun, and then said melodiously:

"Blessed Virgin of Studzianna, forgive me for what I am about to say, but may the Devil break this rotten clay pot!"

She threw her mug on the ground with sorrowful irritation.

"It's a sin, sister, to get so wrathful over a mere piece of ceramic," a brother told her harshly.

"My dear brother, not a year has passed since I paid twenty zlotys for it in Węgrów. Now it's defective and good for nothing."

Resentful, in the midst of the brothers' laughter, she took her butter, which leaked from the rag, and walked away.

I found a place by the puddle, next to a sister who washed her feet and combed her hair and asked a fellow pilgrim:

"Which company are you from, brother?"

"How about you, sister?"

"I'm with the Ciepielów company."

"And I'm with the Zwoleń company."

"That's good, because the Praga company is just a bunch of thieves," she said with deep conviction.

I made no attempt at correcting her; instead, I just went on washing myself as I listened to a conversation between two brothers sitting behind me. One of them said:

"If you can afford pear trees, you'll be able to afford wheat."

"Are you from far away, brother?" the second one asked.

"No, I'm from just outside Warsaw."

"Have you been wearing shoes the whole way?"

"Indeed."

"That's too bad, dear brother."

"I'd rather ruin my shoes than my legs! Let the nobility walk barefoot. We can still afford shoes even though we're just peasants," he said snidely.

"I'm still a noble descended from the nobility, while you, brother, are a peasant and a simpleton."

"A noble who walks barefoot is good for nothing."

"Even if he walks barefoot, a noble is a noble. My brother, I have manners and class and honor, but you, brother, are a boorish, simple man."

"And you, brothers, are classy and delicate people, because, as the saying goes:

A bag of groats, a bag of lard, a bag of flour —
A man from Podlachia can have dessert at any hour."

The noble snorted, but he said snidely:

"If you, brother, were not a coarse person, you would not repeat what fools say, but it's clear that when we ruled you still crawled on all fours and were whipped, my brother."

"And there's a second saying: 'Petty nobility: some steal, others just call it a deal.'"

"You are a boor, a complete boor, my brother!"

And he walked away, keeping his calm.

Crowds of local peasants in exceptionally colorful clothes were hanging around our brothers. The women were dressed in red, while the men wore white homespun coats, red pants, and spencers; their hats were shaped like upside-down milk pails covered in double braids, some of which were velvet.

As I studied these people, a young boy of about eighteen in a blouse, straw hat, and Persian slippers came up to me and asked:

"Are you from Warsaw, brother?"

"Yes."

I saw that this brother had a cherub-like face.

"You wouldn't happen to know, brother, who built this abbey?"

"Alas, I do not."

He said nothing, only sat down with a hiss of pain, took off his slippers, took out a bottle, and began to rub lead water into his swollen and sore feet.

"You won't make it to Czestochowa, brother," I said sympathetically.

"I will. The Virgin Mary will help me, and I will make it, even if it's on all fours," he replied with a tenderly seraphic smile.

He masked his shrewdness with naïveté and looked like a typical momma's boy, so I did not quite believe his sincerity.

I went to the veiled women, who were sitting by the fence. The faces of two-thirds of them were exposed, because Melancholy had not taken off her veil.

Their faces were very kind and pleasant.

We agreed to walk together ahead of the company, because we had a four-mile journey to where we would be spending the night, and it was already two in the afternoon.

Soon enough, we were walking on better sands.

The landscape outside Studzianna drastically differed from that of the town. We walked along dunes where dyer's greenweeds and paltry junipers were growing. There was some rye here and there, but it was very shabby. The horizon was closed off by sand-yellowed hills. The hills were like skulls whose hair had been torn out by windstorms, with just a couple wisps of hair left, the remains of the trees that encircled the dunes from below.

No villages or people were anywhere to be found; a sad and ugly emptiness dominated.

We walked several versts and saw clouds of dust, which led us to conclude that the company was not far behind us. We walked with double our normal strength, but the rest flowed like an avalanche and flooded us in a sparse pine forest, having swam over us like a cloud. We caught up to them again a couple versts later, when there was a break.

We looked for milk and bread; we finally found some, but the peasant did not want to sell it.

"I don't have a wife, so I don't know if I can sell it. If I did, she'd yell at me," he explained.

I wanted to pay him up front, because many people fear hearing "May God reward you" for a good or service.

"I never sold milk, so I don't know how much I should charge," he said as he scratched his rumpled head and spat at intervals.

Ultimately, Contradiction took out a kneading trough, but we had nothing to drink and the ladies had to wash very filthy mugs, which were hanging in two rows on the wall. Finally, he showed that there was only a quart of milk left and he was all out of bread. Nothing could convince the peasant to bring more milk. He had brought a loaf of bread, but he had no scale and could not weight it; I could have paid him anything just to cut a slice. He sent a young boy to the village to borrow a scale and said calmly:

"I want neither to hurt anyone nor be hurt myself," he said as he held a loaf of bread in his hands.

We were forced to wait, although we could see that the company was already departing.

Having eaten, I asked:

"How far away is the nearest church?" It was our tradition that we solemnly marched into every church we encountered on our way, or at least into every church within a one or two-verst radius.

"It'll be a little over one verst."

That "little over one verst" turned out to be four versts of sandy road.

We stepped into a wooden church in a typically peasant fashion, and after a break lasting half an hour or so we took off for Konice.

We had to walk across six versts of sand, sand, sand, and

pebbles to Opoczno. There is a saying: "If across the land of Opoczno you stroll/After each hill and mound, you'll find a knoll." I would say this every time I saw an acre of flimsy wheat. Despite this, the villages were marked by thick, long rows of cherry orchards.

The road was very difficult, and our thirst grew unbearable, but there was not a drop of water to be found.

We often stumbled because there was a myriad of pebbles as sharp as flints. Every so often, the veiled women shook sand out of their moccasins; I could see that they suffered greatly because of these pebbles and because they were very thirsty.

Once again, we were at the very end, even behind the carriages, because our strength was depleting.

As we went through a village, I looked for milk, but with no success; I also looked for water, but again to no avail. The company ahead of us had drunk everything, while the only well in the entire village was somewhere in the middle of a field. Tough luck. I knew we'd eventually find some water, but I felt with a certain amount of fear that every movement caused me increasing pain. Furthermore, the area was hopelessly ugly.

We finally started walking along a hardened plateau surrounded by lovelier wheat fields, which made the landscape more diverse. We asked some pretty and very clean-dressed children who knelt by the road and begged with their glances and their hands, which they had folded as if in prayer.

"How far away is Konice?"

"Over yonder!" they said, pointing to a black forest some five versts away.

We only looked at each other with despair and walked, sweetening this bitterness and exhaustion with candies that one of the sisters had brought with her. There was a minor dispute, because Contradiction was bent on proving that the huge patch of lush green clover on the slope was a pea plant or at least buckwheat.

That was how we fooled hunger and thirst, but there was no way of quelling our hunger.

We rested every half-verst, because Melancholy could barely walk. Through her veil, I saw her mouth bend in pain and that she was almost out of energy.

The sun was setting; it stopped above a wonderfully soft wavy line of hills in the forest. It flamed until it became a completely red and lashless ball, after which it began its descent. I could almost see it fall. The deep valleys in front of us were full of pearly-blue fogs, which were slowly becoming saturated with the purple of the sunset, which initially gave them a lily hue and then a tone of heliotrope with a whitish rim. The wheat fields and trees remained motionless; silence emerged from the darkness and seemed to spin over vast expanses of land and vaporize into increasing silence. The world put on solemn, pensive melancholy, which made it so beautiful that I wanted nothing but to sit, stare at it, and sigh.

Later, everything slowly became blurry, faded, expanded, flattened, and spilled over in the shadows. Every few moments, a bit of forest, hill, or clump of trees would break off, dissolve in the night, and give off a cool breeze. Night was falling, but we were still walking along the fields in silence, along that infinite road that remained white in the dusk.

I was so worn-out that if not for Melancholy, who was walking at the fore, almost unconscious from exertion, I would have lain down on the road and stopped there for the night.

We finally arrived in Konice.

Because the village consisted of only a dozen or so huts, only some of the pilgrims and carriages could spend the night in Konice; the rest went to neighboring villages to sleep. Despair started to get the best of us because we could find neither our carriages nor the rest of the company. Where to look for lodging? And how could we walk further after all our strength had been depleted? The veiled women said that they could even sleep in a ditch because they lacked the strength to go any further. I found a house in a nearby village that seemed less crowded and I barely succeeded in convincing them to go there. I stood in front of the hut and pondered. Where could I go? All the barns, pigpens, and yards were completely swamped with sleeping pilgrims.

My God! I thought to myself as I saw an expanse of a sandy field next to the road. My God! How stupidly civilized I was! I took off my shoes, because they made my feet hurt horribly, and lay down in a furrow. Within a minute, I was sound asleep and had forgotten about everything. I awoke at dawn, right on time.

The air had made me grow very stiff and intoxicated, so I could not rise or even breathe because of an acute pain in my lungs. I somehow managed to get up, though, because everyone from our company was flocking to the cross. Because I had sworn that I would make it to Czesto-chowa despite all odds, I could not allow myself to get sick.

We once again walked across fields and forests with increasing internal momentum and growing persistence.

The sun burned us, the dust choked our breasts, all our body parts were growing heavy from exhaustion, and all the difficulties flayed our bodies, but the pilgrims' eyes and hearts grew brighter because Czestochowa was getting closer.

We were still separated by hills, rivers, empty stretches of sand, terrible roads, and heat, but Czestochowa was setting more and more souls aflame.

I walked along with the crowd because I liked walking with them more and more, as I gradually was coming to understand them better and feel part of them as I forgot about the rest of the world. There was so much to see, hear, and feel all around me that I could not think of anything else.

13

Wielka-Wola

THERE WAS A LARGE CHURCH THAT HAD once been an abbey in this town. Behind the doors, which contained hand forged Baroque arabesques, there was a cemetery circumscribed by simple peasant-style poles, behind which there were brightly painted stations of the cross. This was the work of some master whose specialty was probably embellishing peasants' mailboxes with painted flowers and dragons.

There were a dozen or so stone and iron tombs at the cemetery.

One of them contained the following inscription:

He did not astonish the world with wondrous deeds;
He brought the world consolation — something
much higher indeed.

The luminous and neatly kept church was full of blackened gilding, monstrous statues decorating the altars, portraits, and tombstone plaques on the walls. The church had an absolutely affected, riveting Baroque style.

After Mass, the people crowded in the cemetery and the great sandy square in front of the church.

The sun beat down even more, but hardly anyone noticed; instead, they only slept, ate, and rested in the sand under the sun's rays.

I purchased two glasses of something that was called coffee from a market stall and thought about sleeping, but I gave up that thought upon meeting the veiled women. They had temporarily sat down next to some city slicker and were busy making hot cocoa and unloading part of their provisions.

Jesus! I did not know that it was possible to get provisions like that.

I, who had nothing apart from my suitcase and what I was wearing, grew cold upon seeing the baskets, suitcases, and bundles belonging to these ladies in the carriage. The allure would disappear if I had brought along with me this mass of civilized luxuries. Despite this, I enjoyed drinking the cocoa, which was my first drink since Warsaw that tasted normal and had been prepared for a human to drink.

Afterwards, the seraphic boy appeared and began to walk with us.

Melancholy dubbed this boy Brother Seraph, because he not only constantly spoke about the saints, the sweetness of the priesthood and monastic life, and the visions of saints who appeared to him in his dreams, but his external appearance fit these words. He had bangs and wore an enormous rosary around his neck. He kept a breviary filled with colorful bookmarks under his arm and his pocket was filled with cards with pictures of the saints, prayers, and novenas. The boy spoke in a quiet, sweet, and ecstatic voice; he always looked towards the heavens with tenderness and had the smile and pose of a holy youth.

The ladies were in good spirits, although they looked as if they had just been taken off the cross. An important matter had come up before we left. The carriages and some of the people would walk along the road, which was a longer distance but was of much better quality, while the company would walk along shorter side roads, and we would all meet the following morning in Przedbórz. I was told that that road was hideous, while the surrounding area was not at all interesting. The ladies and I decided to follow the carriages. We could not convince Seraph to go with us, however.

"I will go where the cross is," he said, raising his eyes towards the heavens, and indeed he followed the cross.

As we parted with the brothers, I felt a strange sadness and missed the songs, that sea of heads, and that current that affected and attracted me; I felt the chill of abandonment and emptiness, even though there were about two hundred of us.

The area outside Żarnów, a city that had been rebuilt after a fire, was increasingly hilly and wooded. The road sloped downward, cut across deep valleys, and circled in different directions.

The vicinity of Kołoniec was even wilder. The hills merely formed the horizon and there were few croplands, just forests, thickets, ravines, and low meadows filled with wicker and alders.

There were more and more bodies of water; godforsaken and sunken mineshafts; and roads made of harsh, glassy slag.

In a town whose name I do not remember we saw something resembling a mill, except that in place of stones and wheat there were huge hammers powered by water that processed heated ore. The tall chimneys of a coal plant sharply contrasted with the green trees.

After that, the road was like a slightly elevated causeway. On the left there was a whirlpool of trees, rushes, reeds, and water covered by a layer of greenish rust. On the right was a meadow cut in half by a network of ditches with alder trees growing in them, after which there were hills and forests. The beauty of the raw wilderness had a primeval quality; it seethed with the voices of wild birds and the bubbling of the broad waters.

We rested in Kołoniec, a mining settlement.

Of the three ovens, only one worked; it smelted ore into raw material. We watched this thanks to the kindness of those who supervised the entire process. They smelted only a hundred hundredweights of raw material a day and purchased ore; they explained that it was more convenient and cheaper to buy it at a rate of twenty kopecks a hundredweight than dig in their own soil, even though this made the yield of the raw material even greater.

These buildings and ovens were like islands in a great sphere of waters, swamps, and forests. The soil was black and everything, including the people and plants, seemed saturated by the rust and that dust that came from the slag.

I looked around me and I noticed the young man with tuberculosis from under a lilac bush. He was wrapped up in blankets, while his mother was standing next to a bush by the fence, throwing flower-filled branches onto his knees. She constantly kept asking him:

"Is that enough, Antoś?"

"Just a little more, Mom!" And so, he continued to delightedly caress his face with the flowers.

His eyes were filled with such joy that I moved back on tiptoes so I would not interrupt him.

What a strange soul! It took me a long time to get the specter of that emaciated face radiating with joy out of my brain.

The waves rippled at my feet softly and flowed like aquamarine coils; the lilacs exhaled fragrance; and the light murmur of the waters and forests had such a strange charm that I sat by the riverbank for a long time and fell asleep, rocked by the silence and swimming along with the current across the warmth of the sunshine and the calm....

Some brothers woke me up; I barely had enough time to get some lilacs and we were already on our way. This was only nominally a road, because it had no properties of a road in the normal sense, not even markers to indicate how many versts we had passed. The slag creaked so piercingly under the wheels of the carriage that I ran far ahead so I would not hear it.

We had to walk about five versts through the forest to get to Fałków.

In Fałków, there was a delicious road lined with larches and a very old and simple church, a simple quadrilateral with absolutely no architectural decorations.

We took a fifteen-minute break and went on.

Right before nightfall, we arrived at a village where we would spend the night. All the horses and some of us found lodging in a manor house. We went to see a simply gorgeous new church that had been opened a decade or so ago by Mr. Jakubowski, the owner of Kołoniec, Fałków, and many other villages. Everything from the fencing and the flower-filled cemetery to the church floor betrayed good artistic taste.

I slept nude and in a bed for the first time since Warsaw. I sank and immediately fell asleep in the wonderful comforter they had given me. Parting ways with the comforter was difficult.

As soon as we had left Fałków, we entered a forest that stretched all the way to Przedbórz, which was where we saw the first fields of that day.

The area was very picturesque, although the soil was poor, and the peasants lived in very trashy homes. Everywhere, wheat had been sown on ploughed soil, and although at some points there it was very unstable, there are four little ploughed fields. The wheat was also paltry, and the surrounding villages were falling apart and dirty. The locals were somehow sleepy and silent, and there were plenty of inns in the area.

Some brothers and I started walking together just outside Przedbórz. Our introductions and greetings went on without end. We went into the town together.

14

Przedbórz

THIS WAS A VERY OLD AND UNKEMPT TOWN
with a large Jewish population. It was spread out across the
slope of a stony hill that ran right down to the Pilica River
and sat like a ragged, dirty vendor. The main market square
had very old one-story houses, but there was nothing unique
about them. There were a few arcade-like cellars and a series
of houses whose uninhabited floors were falling apart.

Because there were seven more companies, there was a
huge crowd on the square in front of the ancient church
covered with green moss.

I lacked the strength to look for the church's vestibule,
because the previous day's nearly eight-mile walk started to
take a toll on my body just then.

I looked for a restaurant, but there were none. I only
found a pub with noblemen and the invitation "Come in,
brother!" painted on the sign.

So, I went in.

It was a truly medieval den. The walls were covered with
bright murals depicting scenes of revelry and fun; their
rendition of what it is like to be drunk was sincere.

Two noblemen were painted on one of the walls. Between
them was the following poem:

> *Good day to you, my mate.*
> *Ask them to give you something great.*
> *You can ask away,*
> *But you must pay.*
> *For credit is dead.*

The whole wall was carefully painted with poetry; it was
dotted with big letters and characters.

We left at noon, when the heat was the greatest. We once again crossed the Pilica River and swam in a sea of sand, but not for long, because we once again came across hills. The road led across parched, clay-like soil. Huge, blossoming fields of rapeseed stretched like belts of bright-yellow cloth.

Brother Seraph, who was walking with us, asked with the naiveté of an honest Varsovian:

"What are all those poppies for, brother?"

We burst out laughing, and one sister said snidely:

"They're for making Warsaw cookies, brother."

Seraph turned red and confessed that he did not know how to distinguish between the stem of a potato and rye. The brothers laughed at him a bit, but he again began to sing his trademark song about churches, priests, and Masses, so they gathered around him and walked in silence.

The sun poured fire directly onto our uncovered heads.

We were walking across a very lovely area that could be the source of much material for landscape painters.

Round and proud hills stood in a sunny glory; brooks cut across deep valleys that glimmered from afar; batches of forests and villages were stuck onto the hillside; there were farms in the long passageways between the hills—the goldish green of the wheat covered with rusty stains of freshly-tilled land, yellow fields of rapeseed, and the white walls of houses and the red bricks of manor houses rippled like waves in the sea. Everywhere, the contours were gentle, and the descents and elevations were calm and long, while the profiles were soft, surrounded by sun dust, and shrouded by opaline air.

In the midst of this sumptuous space, the spring, and the sun, the crowd of people sang and walked with the cross at the fore across everything.

At times it seemed to me that these songs formed into specter-like contours, like the transparent shadows of people, and floated in front of us in the golden light of day, like an infinite procession of our souls, which had been woven from radiant material.

15

Wielgomłyny

THE NAME OF THE VILLAGE MEANT NOTHING
to me, because there was only one mill in the creek, which
consisted of water that barely crawled across a patch of sand.
They went to meet us with terribly jangling music.
The church, which had once been an abbey, was over-
loaded with decorations, had blackened with age, and was
covered with musty paintings.

A history of St. Stanislaus, Bishop and Martyr, painted
in a single pearly hue, hung in the presbytery.

The tints and contours broke through the layer of lime-
stone on the roof and walls. It was clear that a painter-
renovator had been there.

The statues were not at all Parthenonian, but the biological sisters of hideous potters' works sold as toys for peasant
children at local farms.

Shortly thereafter, we rested and went to spend the night
in Silnica, which the brothers called Stepmother, because
the peasants there were hesitant to give lodging.

We were graciously offered the manor house chancellery
and a bundle of straw to sleep on. The ladies decided to
sleep in the room, while Seraph and I occupied the vestibule. I was terribly hungry, but my hunger for rest was
even greater, so I sank into the straw; right then, I heard a
brother quietly singing Vespers.

I waited until he was done, which I knew would happen. Indeed, he stopped singing Vespers, but then he began
singing something else.

I was forced to spend the night outside the house. Dogs
that had been unleashed for the night hungrily tried to
snatch my sausage, which I suddenly had to fight for. They
mellowed out and calmly lay next to me.

There was such great silence, the nightingales sang so sweetly in the thickets, the lilacs smelled so lovely, and the moon shone so wonderfully that I could not even entertain the thought of sleeping.

The dogs did not even nap; their yellowish eyes glistened, they growled silently and protractedly, and they lay next to me with their heads raised.

Exhaustion, the pain in my legs, and even hunger departed me. I relished the silver-violet fragrance of the lilacs and the charm of the May night. I lay motionless for hours on end in the dew-bronzed grass awash with the moonlight.

I began to wander, half-asleep. It seemed to me that the trees in the park were beginning to tremble, blend together, and become clothed in bodies, and so the depths, sprinkled with silver, became populated by specters and the fogs that strutted above the grass, curling and surrounding all the shadows in the fluttering veils and the whole throng of specters that constantly fell apart and ran off again. They seemed to become one in the thousands of iterations of Melancholy's face and began to walk, ascending an elevated surface and descending once again, while the songs that I had heard over so many days began to ring in my brain and resound louder and louder amid the silence.

It seemed to me that I was walking, that I had passed a swarm of barely perceptible forms and colors, that the sun was simultaneously rising and setting, and that I was flowing faster and faster. . . .

I had neither the strength nor the will to break out of this procession of the nightmares of my tired brain.

The roosters began to crow, and the world became cloudy. I went to the vestibule and the dogs followed me, but before I could get warm in the straw it was time to get up and go again.

The songs resounded once again, the cross was at the fore of the company, and we walked past forests, villages, wheat fields, and brooks. We pushed forward like an unshackled force to the magnetic field that rested in every brain and every heart, growing more profuse and having an increasingly strong impact.

I could no longer hear chitchat or jokes. The songs were sung more zealously and by greater numbers of pilgrims.

Near every cross, pilgrims crawled through dust, kissing not only the cross but also picket fences and the stones that lay below them.

Bodies disappeared, and only the features and expressions of faces remained, while eyes were becoming more feverishly aflame. Individuals grew silent and merged together. You could no longer see differences between the nobility, peasants, and burghers, or between men and women; all converged into one glowing wave of religious exultation.

During breaks, they would fall onto the ground like wood blocks; they would quickly get up, walk, and sing after the first ring of the bell.

Most lived off the dry bread that they carried on their backs. Nobody cared if they ate, slept, were sick, or if it was hot or cold; they simply fell, got back up, and walked with even greater intensity.

As I write these words, I feel that I have entered the same orbit as they, that I am gravitating towards the same center. I napped under that benevolent sun, eating what I had if there was anything to eat; I walked like everyone, sang, and listened and looked more often. When they asked, I would respond. When they demanded something, I would give it if I had it. I no longer ate anything or drank tea. Although I no longer had any, I did not knock on doors to look for bread and tea, because I knew that the sister or brother next to me, everyone around me whose friendly glances I often felt, would be quick to bring me a slice of bread in the name of brotherhood.

I let myself go with the current and swam. Where to? I did not ask, because I was happy. I felt that I was increasingly becoming part of them. I had entered into a kind of warm, mystical kinship with these souls and felt the same as they about the simplest things. The pleasure of movement, freely breathing in the clean air, the joy of resting in the open air, the animal-like delight of eating anything; those same strange goosebumps upon seeing priests, churches, beautiful ceremonies, and gildings — tears poured down my face just as they did down theirs and the same spasm of tender emotion tugged at my heart when I heard the solemn sounds of organs, when the dark chill of churches wrapped around me, and when priests used certain impassioned expressions in their speech: God . . . punishment . . . virtue . . . hell . . . Amen, they would say with pompous voices.

Exhaustion and the sameness of my impressions so painted my sensitivity that I could not comprehend many things; I forgot about many things and became indifferent to others. I had become so tired that I did not mind that nobody knew me and nobody asked who I was; I was nothing, a unit, a brother, one number in the general list of pilgrims, not a Mr. X. or Mr. Y. who could not show himself without the mask of a civilized brother.

I was not even a will, but a certain sum of muscles put into automatic motion with persistently intensified sensuality. I was only one pulse of that one heart with four thousand heads. Nobody here even had the mask of a name.

Who could enchant me here and with what, amid the hypnosis that the aim of the journey produced? If I got sick, they would put me on a carriage and carry me. If I became poor, they would feed me without ostentatious philanthropy, gather their faded groszy, and give them to me; they would do this with simplicity and sincerity. If I were to die, I would like to be buried at some roadside cemetery where there are as many green birch trees and as much chirping of birds as there. They would build a burial mound, plant a weeping willow, and whenever they would pass the grave in springtime they would throw a branch of blackthorn or bundle of forest pasqueflowers, while I would sleep silently and dream sweetly until eternity, living on in their hearts and memories longer than in the marketplace of the world.

At times I forgot who I was, and it seemed to me that I had always lived like that and always would do so.

Is happiness not inner peace? Is it not contemplation, the silvery fog into which man slowly sinks, forgetting about everything, which allows him to be indifferently carried by the waves of fate to wherever he likes?

I caught myself being sentimental and began to speak soberly.

Enough.

16

Cielętniki

THIS WAS A TINY VILLAGE WITH A CHURCH where we stopped to rest. Bread and milk helped me to recover my strength somewhat, while the tea I drank at the presbytery reinvigorated my spirits.

The finished church was red and had Gothic steeples. It was built thanks to two-groszy donations that the local parish vicar had been persistently collecting from pilgrims for twelve years, as this was a poor and very small parish.

There was an enormous linden, several hundred years old, in the cemetery. The peasants looked at it with a kind of veneration and whispered:

"Oh, Lordy! What a giant!"

Portraits of knights and matrons had been transferred from the old church to the presbytery, where they served as a pretty decoration in the hallway. Those covered in steel plates and the girls in ball gowns looked at a flock of chicks bathing in sand and the crowds freely swarming next to them.

We left at ten. The sun scorched as if it were July.

17

Dąbrowa

THIS WAS A GORGEOUS LITTLE TOWN. DIF-
ferent elements of the church were of such different styles
that none gave it a unique flavor, but the interior was very
pretty and very neatly maintained. The statues were even
tolerable.

Next to the choir were bas reliefs from seventeenth and
eighteenth-century graves that were exceptionally tough in
their manufacture. In the narthex, meanwhile, there was a
plaque proclaiming that the church had been restored to
its present state thanks to the generosity of the Schleiber
and Herbst families, in whose intentions the faithful were
asked to pray. There was a delicious lawn and very pretty
stations of Christ's Passion at the cemetery.

I saw that there were lots of people huddled by a statue
next to the church. They watched it in pious concentration
and had a certain fear in their faces, while their voices were
subdued.

I also looked at it. This statue was purely secular in
nature and dated back to the age of Louis XV; it was a
bucolic stone statue in the style of Watteau. It was some
crowned marquis in pompous dress and some dame with
a pompadour-style hairdo sitting in the grass and apparently whispering tender and sweet words, flirting in an
eighteenth-century style. They were clearly descended
from a race of bored and genteel sophisticates. In terms of
expression and execution, the statue was completely banal;
besides, rain and frost had caused erosion. The stone was
peeling and falling off, while grass grew in a crevice in
the statue's hips. Nobody could tell me where this statue
had come from. I did, however, hear the following legend
from some sister:

"This was a long time ago. A woman had two children, a boy and a girl. She liked to drink a bit and gossip with her gal friends and visit her neighbors. Meanwhile, her children did whatever they wanted. With a mother like that, it's no surprise that they were licentious pests. One time, she drank a little more than usual. When she had arrived at her house, the children were gone.

"When they finally came back, the drunk woman had lost her reason and went completely mad and beat the girl with a stick and tried to hit the boy, too. The boy didn't let her, though, so he grabbed a broom and hit his mother on the head with it. She became even angrier and struck his mouth, but the boy only fell. The woman was completely under the influence of liquor, so she sat and lamented, saying: 'Why don't they just die and turn to stone!'

"She said this until she saw that the children who had embraced and wept from pain somehow grew black and sat somewhat stiff; their eyes became motionless, but pearls fell down their cheeks. Fear sobered up the woman, so she ran to them, but the children were cold as stones, while their eyes were still open and wept and wept. She lamented, people came, the priest came, too, and they then brought someone who knew about these things, but nothing happened. The children had turned to stone. They did not bury them, because how can you bury a stone that constantly cries? They put them in front of the church.

"The woman was overcome with woe; she did not eat or sleep, she only sat day and night and waited until her beloved children would change. Years passed, but nothing happened. She prayed so much, cried so much, and bought so many Masses for this intention! She asked God to die, but death did not come.

"One time, she crawled on all fours to Czestochowa and asked the Blessed Mother to have mercy and turn her into a birch tree that would immediately grow in that hole, soaking from the children's sobs, so that she could always be by them and at least protect them from the sun and the rain with her branch. Eventually, though, the tears stopped flowing and the birch tree withered. The Lord Jesus pardoned her curses and took her and her children to His glory."

18

St. Anne's Outside Przyrów

WE WALKED THE SIX VERSTS FROM DĄBROWA very quickly, because we had crossed a road, a forest, and meadows that were buttressed by trees on both sides.

There was a great crowd and much commotion in front of the church, because the Łowicz company was coming right behind us, while several other companies were arriving from other sides. The Łowiczaks were a sturdy and beautiful people; their former prosperity was evident in their faces and their dress. Their costumes were marvelous. The women were very pretty, and they were all clad in crimson, which speckled our grayness like poppies. All wore boots with red ribbons and coral necklaces, and they held white handkerchiefs in their hands. The men wore red pants in white, yellow, and green transverse stripes. They wore navy-blue bonnets circumscribed by red cords, pointed hats, and red ribbons in their shirts.

The church was big and pretty. St. Anne's Chapel was lovely, and its interior was in the purest Baroque style. The high altar was wonderful.

We could not enter the convent, because it was inhabited by ten Dominican sisters.

We left at three in the afternoon and still had thirty-one versts to Mstów, where we would spend the night.

Everyone was tired on that penultimate day.

I could not hold a pencil in my hand, because the moment I sat sleep irresistibly clawed at me, and even when it did not, I felt so internally defeated and confused that I could not pull a single thought, sentence, or image out of me. Sleep was all I was capable of doing.

We began the thirty-one versts walking past an avenue of poplar trees, half of which had broken and toppled, as a big storm had passed through there and thrown these giants to the ground like wood chips. Next, there was some forest, sands, villages, barren land, and again, *da capo*, the same thing over.

Although the singing of the bunch, always equally dormant, kept us awake, and a force or momentum tried to pull us towards them, we were increasingly far behind the company.

For about an hour, we still saw it; it seemed almost like a hallucination, because we were barely conscious.

The veiled women clenched their mouths and seemed to attach to the increasingly distant silhouettes with their stares, shuffling with what remained of their nerves.

The Łowicz company had caught up to us, after which the Zwoleń company passed us; like a blue cloud, they hung above us and then disappeared. The Ciepielów company had arrived and several smaller ones came as well, but we dragged like the sediment of this human stream that moved forward with such power.

It seemed to me that we were sliding further into a kind of grayness, pushed by those who were stronger.

Right after the forest, we asked: how far away is Mstów? They said it was six versts away.

By the time we had walked six versts, we asked again. This time, they said it was eight versts away. So, we no longer asked anyone. We met some Łowiczaks who had already prepared for the night in an overcrowded village. One of the women sitting by the road counseled Melancholy:

"Sister, why don't you take off these shoes and walk the rest of the way barefoot? It'll be easier."

"They're coming off themselves!" said a peasant who saw what had remained of her moccasins.

I was no longer irritated by their laughter. On leaving the village, we entered a grassland full of sand and rocks.

A strong gust of wind whipped our faces with bright sand.

Night was falling, but it was somehow dirty, and the bare, rocky hills that were devoid of any plant life and the barren lands seethed sadly.

Neither the stars nor the moon could be seen, only the maelstrom of the grayness that swirled around us.

Tossed around by the windstorm, telegraph wires moaned pathetically above us.

Completely exhausted, we walked in silence.

We encountered neither villages nor people. At times it seemed to us that the echoes of singing came along with the windstorm and that we could already see lights inside human dwellings and the silhouettes of brothers. That was only an illusion, however. The wind only whistled and scurried clouds of dust, while partridges called to one another across the fields.

My legs were lacerated, and at every step there was a pile of small but sharp stones, and I could see no end of the barren land. I felt silent wrath at my own physical powerlessness and my helpless pain since I could help neither myself nor Melancholy, who was hunching over lower and lower like a ripe ear of grain.

We finally arrived at some mill from which we still had two versts left to walk.

"We will make it," she said softly; I sensed a touch of calm determination in her voice.

Seraph was already praying in some exceptionally weepy and powerless voice, but we kept walking on those stones and finally arrived at the abbey, where the mother and the rest of the company were supposed to be.

There was nothing to be found in the labyrinth of corridors that was literally stuffed with people.

They were sleeping everywhere; there were tons of people on the stairs, in the cemetery, and even by the road and in ditches.

There was nothing. That day, nobody was singing. I saw pilgrims sleeping with books opened on their knees, saying almost the last word of their evening prayers. Some were holding their rosaries in their hands while sleeping and sitting by the fences with loaves of bread they had begun to eat and with opened bundles; the snoring was the only indication that everyone was asleep.

It was going to rain, because the clouds were piling up and dragging on ponderously, while a sudden quiet was fluttering.

I went to the priest's housekeeper to ask for just a tiny piece of the floor as long as it was under a roof.

"There's no more room."

The servant softly told her about an empty room.

"Wait a moment!" the housekeeper said. "Never mind; there's underwear hanging all over the room, and I don't have the time to fold it. Besides, since you've decided to make the sacrifice to go to Czestochowa, it won't be a problem for you to sleep outside." An ironic smile twisted her face.

We finally ran into people from our company. We would spend the night in a little den where thirty people were already sleeping.

It was so cramped that even if it was possible to find a place to rest one's head, finding room for one's legs was out of the question.

I heard Seraph promise some sister holy cards, prayers, and finally money if she budged just a little, but it was to no avail. The air in the room was so stuffy that it would have been safer to spend the night under a carriage in the main market square.

The excitement that it was the last day was evident on everyone's face.

When we pushed across the empty streets of Mstów, in the sunrise I noticed some blood stains on the cobblestone: they had been made by those who were walking ahead of us, singing and marking the cobblestone with their bare feet.

We came upon some truly hilly roads. The sun was rising, but it immediately drowned in the fog, making it only slightly purple. The paths were steep and filled with sharp stones. The area was hilly and bald peaks poked out of the morning fog.

We walked so quickly that everyone wheezed. At every peak and elevation, everyone's eyes got lost in the fog. Anxious, zealous stares looked for the outline of the Czestochowa tower in the grayish clouds.

They paused and stood with outstretched arms for a moment.

I could see nothing; the whole world seemed to have sunk in this moving mass.

At once, a strange shiver flew past the crowd.

The sun was rising above the fog and a shadow appeared and quickly faded like a proud phantasm ahead of us, because the fog rolled up as if it had been struck by the power of light, swirled, and fell out like feathers, covering everything.

Something like a moan of disappointment rustled, and something like a fierce battle between the crowd and the fog broke out.

Feverish stares with bloody glimmers of exhaustion, accelerated heartbeats, all the heightened senses, and all the voices that had grown hoarse from intensification, all combined together and flowed in a stream of fire, saturating the fog and drinking from it, all the while becoming increasingly sparse.

These goosebumps that constantly penetrated us blinded and hypnotized the crowd so much that we continued to move forward.

There were more and more bloody imprints on the ground and on the rocks, but those who made them continued walking, paying no attention to their pain and the blood flowing from their legs: the proximity of the aim gave them strength.

We stopped at the Hill of Forgiveness.

Some brothers gave the final speeches. Whispers of exoneration could be heard among the pilgrims. The voice that was giving a speech dully resounded in the fog, but hardly anyone listened to it. Everyone's ears, eyes, and hearts were elsewhere.

We nearly ran down this very steep hill and once again there was this exasperating shiver....

The sun continued rising and that specter of the tower, probably a reflection, seemed to have broken off from its fundaments and for a moment hovered over the vapors and rocked, its peak shining until another and final wave of fog again hid it.

Finally, we stood on the last hill and instantly began to stare as the clouds contracted in layers, swirling and moving tearing upwards. Finally, the air was clear, and all eyes focused on the big hill with a tower on top.

Yells of "Mary!" burst like fire from a thousand breasts, while a thousand bodies fell on the ground with shouts of joy. Like a cyclone, this sight turned all these heads to dust.

"Mother!" voices choking on happiness and ecstasy called. Tears of joy began to flow, while eyes radiated with love. Everyone shook while sobbing, which greatly moved the heart, and there was not a soul or a will that did not prostrate in tearful delight.

Those sobs quickly turned into moans, nearly into a roar, flooding brains and hearts and fusing into one solid mass, trembling in its sobs and becoming a single feeling. It freed everyone of sadness, pain, the bitterness of existence, all the expressions of misery, and everything they had suffered from all those hearts, flowing to the feet of the One whom every heart saw, to the feet of Goodness and Consolation.

Through its rhythm of sobs, pleas, and enthusiasm, that deep, simply divine simplicity resounded in the air for a long time, wrapping around all the bodies, burning them like a fiery windstorm and forging the soul anew.

They got up and all the faces suddenly grew sunny, intensifying in their expression.

They sang a song to the Mother of God and walked with the strength of luminosity in their eyes, with smiles on their thin faces, filled with the traces of fatigue, while the triumphant accents of that hymn, broad as the world, rang like the bronze of the hearts and palpitated above the sunny springtime earth.

After one of the Pauline fathers gave a speech, we went into the Jasna Góra church.

I cannot write anything here about what I had experienced; I will leave for myself what I felt there.

I slept for sixteen hours without waking.

After I had bathed and changed my clothes and shoes, I walked out and saw all the brothers and the continual influx of people, which made me feel great sorrow that this journey had come to an end, that we would all soon fall off this mighty mass like leaves in autumn and never come together again; I felt growing aversion to the prospect of going back to the yoke of everyday life, to that mundane mill of urban and civilized life.

Once again, I would have to stand in a line of people distinguished by numbers and last names. Once more, people would have to call me "sir" and I would have to be careful to not upset anyone; I would have to have a top hat in hand and wear a mask over my face.

On Sunday, I saw Melancholy in the penumbra of the monastery choir; she was kneeling and steeped in prayer. Her black clothing added a raw shadow to her beautiful and sad face. The depths of her bluish eyes were filled with silence and benevolence; tears streamed down her pale face and her lips feverishly whispered something. Behind her were hundreds of outspread people weeping in the same way, while souls also moaned and begged with their tears at the bottom.

Later, we all visited the abbey. These were sunny moments.

We were supposed to leave on Monday. I awoke earlier and went to see Mass in the chapel of the Virgin Mary and the moment when the miraculous image would be uncovered.

It was extremely crowded; the people had clung together so closely that it was difficult to detach from them. Every couple minutes, people who had been trampled or had fainted were carried out.

Mass had begun.

The spiral and seemingly goldish vibration of the soft pitches of flutes poured into the silence and seduced souls like a sparkling net. Next, fiddles permeating the singing voices rose in a song full of feeling and vaporized like the fragrance of roses, while organs resounded softly and distantly like the whoosh of the ocean that slowly beats on and brims over the banks, after which it silently seethes and increases in strength, roaring amidst a storm that throws exploding thunderbolts, which funnel through the frightened brass trumpets. The chaos of a somehow shoreless sorrow rages, sobs, and pleads until the flutes call in the pianos and tender, sweet singing like an angelic choir. It flows under the chapel's roof; like consolation, it permeates souls with tenderness and rocks them with words of grace, growing silent in a sudden, brief silence of Exultation interrupted only by the harsh sound of bells like steel splendor.

A song arose from all the instruments at once; a hurricane of shouts and sighs broke from all the hearts. Tangled, crumpled, and annihilated, they all fell to the ground before the uncovered image of the Virgin Mary. A girl held by her mother shoved through that wall of bodies. She walked on crutches and her eyes were closed; she stretched her arms out and called in a voice powerful with the inexpressible sound of her faith:

"Mary, heal me! Mary, heal me!"

She fell onto the ground like a tree that had been cut down, but she immediately got up without crutches. Erect and radiant, she called:

"Mary! I see! Mary! I'm walking!"

She walked towards the altar, while the storm of a nearly inhuman roar burst out of all the hearts and ran to Mary's feet with the love of the newly healed.

The girl walked on, taking off like a bird getting ready for flight with a smile of inexpressible gratitude and her eyes blue like cornflowers; she gasped words of thanksgiving with her arms stretched out; she was overcome by joy, tears, and enthrallment.

"Mary!" Mary!" She fell to her knees, embraced stones with her arms, and clung to them with her pale lips under the feet of the One who sat there sweetly and calmly, holding Jesus on her hand, and was full of clemency and love.

All the people lay praising God's kindness and begging for mercy in their moans, tears, minds, blood, and love.

The church seemed to open its gates in order to let in the crowds of souls that infinitely rushed forward in prayer. A blue veil seemed to flutter above everyone and engulf everything, which some white hands and radiant eyes blessed, consoling, calming, and invigorating hearts, bringing them oblivion and the strength to persist.

Those throngs of people became more and more immersed in their sobs and they seemed to float off to the transcendent sphere on the waves of music that, like the Archangel of Consolation, went forward and carried all souls to the place from where they had come: to the source of goodness and joy. . . .

Wolbórka, May 3, 1894

ABOUT THE AUTHOR

WŁADYSŁAW REYMONT was born in 1867 in Kobiele Wielkie in Russian-ruled Poland. Reymont's work was very diverse, encompassing socially-conscious prose critical of both Dickensian capitalism and Bolshevism, fables, journalism, and even horror. In 1924, he won the Nobel Prize for his four-part novel *The Peasants*, a masterpiece of literary Naturalism which describes the social conventions of nineteenth century Polish peasants and their dependence on the whims of nature. *The Peasants* is still required reading in Polish high schools today, and it was also the basis for a classic 1972 television miniseries. Władysław Reymont died in 1925 and is buried at the Alley of the Distinguished in Warsaw's Powązki Cemetery.

CPSIA information can be obtained
at www.ICGtesting.com
Printed in the USA
LVHW080806310720
661951LV00006B/95